There has been much dissection of modern Indian history, and some gross distortions. But we now have a book which does an honest and cerebral introspection of what India did wrong in the first seven decades of its independence. From leaving Kashmir as a festering wound to ceding territory to China to choosing socialism, state control, and a corrupt license raj, noted business journalist Aarnab Mitra's book crisply lists not just the first PM Jawaharlal Nehru biases and follies but also their ramifications down the years. Aarnab's is a book to read and learn from for the new India.

—Abhijit Majumder
Journalist, Media Entrepreneur, and
Author of *India's New Right*

The *Wasted Decades 1947–1991* is a fascinating book where Aarnab Mitra examines how Nehru's wrong economic policies of socialism and an unwillingness to accept economic freedom of the citizens of a newly independent nation diminished India. India has been a trading free market, rich economy for very large period of its history. Socialism created a cycle of never-ending poverty destroying the future of three generations of Indians. India became poorer by 1991 relative to other nations, which freely participated in the post-War boom and high growth, despite being the most industrialised country in Asia in 1947, as the rest of Asia lay in ruins due to the war. This book is a warning to all Indians to never ever give up our economic freedoms to intellectually arrogant political leaders who try to impose their will on us.

—T.V. Mohandas Pai
Chairman, Aarin Capital Partners

The *Wasted Decades 1947–1991* is a brilliant book and must be read by anyone who wants to understand what went wrong in our nation's journey. More importantly, it must be read to make sure we do not walk on the same path, for we will most surely repeat the same journey; a journey that will ultimately lead us nowhere.

—Dr Anand Ranganathan
Author and Scientist

Incisive and critical analysis of India's economic journey and policy choices—the roads taken and not taken—in the period before the liberalisation of 1991.

—Ashok Malik
Partner, The Asia Group

India, used as it is to growth since the 1990s, seems to have forgotten how desperate and harrowing the 50s, 60s and 70s were. That is why this book is a must read. Aarnab masterfully reminds us of how things were bad and usually got worse; entirely because of doubling down on bad policy choices, refusing to learn from mistakes, and a callous disregard of results. This was reinforced by relying on a coterie of quack academics who concocted empirics and crony industrialists who were protected at the cost of genuine talent. This is the story of how a newly independent India crushed the nascent buds of industrialisation that had emerged towards the end of British rule, in a manner that was far more calculated, vicious and systematic—outdoing the rapaciousness of the British.

—Abhijit Iyer-Mitra
Senior Fellow, IPCS

If there ever was a book that explains how India failed its citizenry in its initial years it is *The Wasted Decades*. The author Aarnab Mitra has brilliantly narrated how bad policy decisions by India's "founding intellectuals" led to a litany of first and second order effects that thwarted India's growth story. The after effects of those decisions can be felt even today as we hobble towards our goal of becoming a $10-trillion economy.

Kushal Mehra
Author and Host of The Cārvāka Podcast

The WASTED DECADES

1947 TO 1991

Dear Reader,

Best wishes,

Aarnab Mitra

AARNAB MITRA

गरुड

Published by
Garuda Prakashan Private Limited
Gurugram, Bharat

www.garudalife.in

First published in Bharat 2025

ISBN: 978-81-994386-4-4

Printed in Bharat

To

My dear friend Ramdas Menon,
who remains fiercely loyal to the ancien régime
and convinced of its success,
despite compelling evidence to the contrary.

Contents

Preface

I grew up in a staunchly Congress family. Our ties with the party go back to before Independence when my maternal grandfather, late Bidhu Bhushan Sarkar, was an influential councillor in the Calcutta Municipal Corporation in the 1920s; he retained his seat till after Independence. Back then, this was among the few elected positions open to Indians. He was a close colleague of stalwart leaders like Subhash Chandra Bose, Dr Bidhan Chandra Roy, and Shyama Prasad Mukherjee.

A few years after his death, one of my maternal uncles, late Pradip Kumar Sarkar, was elected Congress councillor from what came to be considered the family's pocket borough. He was re-elected councillor for several terms till that constituency became a reserved one—except during the phase when elections to CMC were suspended for a long time. Another uncle reached greater heights and became a prominent minister in the Siddhartha Shankar Ray government from 1972 until 1977. In 1998, my family's political allegiance shifted to the Trinamool Congress, which emerged as the primary vehicle to take on the CPI(M)-led Left Front.

My maternal uncle also unsuccessfully contested the 1977 election to the West Bengal Assembly from Manicktala and the 1980 Lok Sabha polls from Contai as a Congress (I) candidate. From his campaign material, I "stole" an Indira Gandhi poster, in which she looked radiant and regal in a cream saree with a saffron–red border. That poster would remain pasted on my bedroom wall for the next decade, alongside the posters of my other heroes, Sunil Gavaskar and Amitabh Bachchan.

In many Bengali households back then, it was the norm to hang small photographs of Rabindranath Tagore, Swami Vivekananda, Netaji Subhash Chandra Bose, and Ramakrishna Paramahansa. Mine was no different. But there was one more photograph in my parents' bedroom—that of Jawaharlal Nehru.

Like the rest of the family, my parents were die-hard Congress supporters and great fans of Nehru and Indira Gandhi. Because politics was often discussed whenever relatives came over, I grew up as a committed Congress supporter. It was and it remains the most natural political affiliation for any child in our family though no one from my generation has entered politics.

The rationale was simple. Wasn't Nehru the architect of modern India? Didn't his Temples of Modern India transform a poor and destitute country into an industrial power that the West was trying hard to keep down? Didn't he give us the IITs, ISRO, BARC, and all the other scientific breakthroughs in agriculture and other fields that Indian News Reels, short publicity films, which mostly showcased the government's achievements and which were mandatorily screened at every film hall before the movie, told us were making India great?

And Indira Gandhi? She was Ma Durga personified—she had single-handedly vanquished Pakistan in 1971, got the better of the evil Nixon–Kissinger duo, and made India a global power by exploding an atom bomb, hadn't she?

Nehru and his daughter were leading India to its tryst with its glorious destiny. They had given all of us self-respect, and were keeping the ubiquitous "foreign hand" at bay.

This was drilled into us in a variety of ways—at school, on special days via carpet bombing of advertisements, in Indian News Reels shorts, and by word of mouth at home.

It was all very rosy and inspirational.

If only it were also true.

Effective censorship ensured that nothing outside the official narrative reached the masses. Radio was a government monopoly; so, it broadcast only what the government wanted people to hear. TV was still out of reach for a vast majority of Indians; in any case, this medium, too, was under stifling government control. Abysmally poor literacy rates kept newspapers out of reach of all but a small section of the urban and semi-urban middle class. Their dependence on government advertising for survival kept them on a leash for the most part. Then, very few Indians could afford to travel abroad and see for themselves where we stood compared to the rest of the world.

This ensured that the news of how far India had begun to lag behind not only the West but also its Asian peers didn't reach anyone apart from a tiny sliver at the top of the social and economic pyramid.

I remember watching a programme on Doordarshan on Rajiv Gandhi's family, shortly after he became the Prime Minister. It was basically an introduction to Rahul and Priyanka Gandhi and their dogs. The unstated subtext of the programme was, "Meet your future PM." Also aired was a film on Rajiv Gandhi by Simi Garewal in which Vishwanath Pratap Singh's rebellion was termed "*vishwasghat*," subliminally reinforcing the point that had been driven into us ad nauseum—that the Nehru–Gandhis were the natural rulers of India and anyone challenging them was an interloper and a betrayer. I was in college then and cheered these programmes with the rest of my friends. We were, after all, products of our times.

My rose-tinted opinion of the Nehru–Gandhi dynasty began to crack when I went abroad for the first time and saw for myself how far behind we had fallen compared to the rest of Asia.

When I returned and aired my views, my boss, whose political leanings I wasn't aware of, stoutly defended India's growth trajectory. "Look at the obstacles Nehru and Indira Gandhi had to overcome. Lesser men (and women) would have thrown in the towel. But it is their indefatigable energy and vision that have got us so far," he said.

I wasn't entirely convinced but gave his argument the benefit of the doubt. Those were the days before internet. There wasn't much material available to read up. The few academic papers I could find were too obtuse, jargon-heavy, boring and, therefore, unreadable.

Meanwhile, I had the privilege of travelling to more foreign destinations, and each trip further cemented my view that we'd been led up the garden path by our leaders and those in charge of disseminating information.

It was only after the broadband internet boom about a decade-and-a-half ago that I could resume my research with vigour. Several Indian and foreign publications and reports, and interviews with leading economists and policy makers in India and abroad became accessible to ordinary readers like me.

I lapped up this information and arrived at the conclusion that my initial impression on my first foreign visit had been justified. I still hadn't thought of writing this book. That came while reading Princeton University professor Ashoka Mody's seminal book *India Is Broken*. While reading, I would often call out to my wife to say: "See, I told you this… Now you have corroboration from an unimpeachable source."

As the number of such corroborations grew, my wife said: "Why don't you write a book yourself?"

That was two years ago. I began by re-reading Nehru's *The Discovery of India*, *Letters from a Father to a Daughter*, *Glimpses of World History*, and *An Autobiography*. My father had made me read all of them when I was in college, but I wanted to refresh my fading memory of those books. I also read books and articles on Nehru and his descendants. I began with Tavleen Singh's *Durbar*, S.S. Gill's *The Dynasty*, Gurcharan Das' *India Unbound*, and Neerja Chowdhury's *How Prime Ministers Decide*. I also read Sharmishtha Mukherjee's book on her father and Ramachandra Guha's *Verdicts on Nehru: The Rise and Fall of a Reputation*. My research also led me to the development journeys of Japan, Taiwan, South Korea, Singapore, and Hong Kong. I read up as much as I could on how their leaders had led them from the Third World to the First.

I will remain eternally grateful to all these books and their authors for giving me varied but very insightful perspectives on the subject I was researching.

In addition to these, I scoured the internet for any reports and analyses I could find of the Indian economy as well as those of its peers between 1947 and 1991. Over a period of time, this became an all-consuming obsession as I came across more information that gave me a better understanding of the issues that our leaders had to confront during that time and of their responses to them. I remain eternally indebted to the many authors and analysts whose wisdom I have greedily partaken of. I have cited those from whom I've borrowed facts and opinions but would also like to say that there were many more who influenced my thinking without contributing anything concrete.

I discovered that all the analyses of India's post-independence economic trajectory focused on the problems and challenges that Nehru and Indira Gandhi had to confront when they assumed office. These were, without an iota of doubt, Himalayan in their proportions, and it is to their credit that they did not cave in under the pressure of the task.

But it is equally true that both of them missed massive opportunities because of their ideological blinkers and their stubborn refusal to change course when it became apparent from the late 1950s onwards that their development and economic mantras were not working. In particular, India completely missed out on the global boom that lasted more than two decades from 1950–1973, which came to be called the Golden Age of Capitalism. India missed out on this opportunity because of Nehru's ideological aversion to foreign trade, which he considered inherently exploitative and a tool for colonialism.

This and other mistakes and missed opportunities are described in the pages that follow.

In addition to all the well-known authors that I have mentioned above, I also owe a huge debt of gratitude to my school and college friends, Namit Shah and Jatin Budhdeo, my Columbia Business School batchmate Prahalad Karnam, and my sister-in-law Priya Das for reading through parts of the early versions of this manuscript and suggesting improvements and/or other changes. These have made the manuscript more readable and easier to grasp.

A special thanks to my friends Ashok Malik and Abhijit Majumder for writing glowing endorsements for this book. I would also like to gratefully acknowledge and thank T.V. Mohandas Pai, Dr Anand Ranganathan, Kushal Mehra, and Abhijit Iyer-Mitra for the very positive endorsements they have written for this book.

I also take this opportunity to thank my wife, Tapa Tanushree Mitra, without whose unstinted and consistent support this book wouldn't have seen the light of day.

Finally, I wish to thank Mangesh Joshi, my editor at Garuda Prakashan, for the wonderful job he has done correcting my many careless errors and citation slip-ups. Thanks also to Jitender Nigam for the lovely cover design, which has significantly enhanced the attractiveness of this book. My appreciation also goes to Krish Harikrishnan, the

Publishing Manager, for patiently answering my incessant phone calls on a variety of issues and addressing my many queries and, most importantly, to K. Hema, Senior Publishing Manager, for guiding me through the entire publication process.

And, above all, I would like to offer my humble homage at the feet of my *ishta devi* Ma Durga, whose presence and blessings I have felt and continue to feel every moment of my life.

Ya Devi sarvabhuteshu maatrurupena samsthita,
Namastasyai namastasyai namastasyai namo namah.

Aarnab Mitra
August 8, 2025

1

A Costly Mistake

It was ultimately the decision of one man that sealed the deal—and ensured that Jawaharlal Nehru, and not Vallabhbhai Patel, came to occupy the position of the first Prime Minister of independent India. Mohandas Karamchand Gandhi was widely acknowledged as a saint. He was, without an iota of doubt, the tallest leader of India's freedom struggle. But that one decision to overrule the popular mandate and foist his own choice on the Congress party, and, in effect, the people of free India, set in motion a series of events that, contrary to the Mahatma's expectations and his political disciple's desired goals, perpetuated poverty, illiteracy, darkness and destitution for at least two generations of Indians, even as other newly independent Asian nations forged ahead on the world stage, leaving India far behind. As Ashoka Mody writes in his book *India Is Broken*, "If Patel had become India's first Prime Minister or if he had lived longer as Nehru's deputy, post-Independence India would have taken a very different shape."[1]

Patel had been the overwhelming choice of the people, or at least those eligible to elect the next president of the Indian National Congress in April 1946. Just prior to this, the British Indian government, then on its last legs, had held elections to the central and provincial assemblies. The elected members would be the leaders of newly independent India. As expected, the Indian National Congress won large majorities in most of these provincial elections. It was helped in no small measure by Patel's organisational ability and command over the rank and file of the Congress organisation.

That year, the election of the Congress president was particularly important because the party chief would be anointed Vice President of the Viceroy's Executive Council, lead India to independence, and become the first Prime Minister of the country. Patel was the overwhelming choice of the majority. As many as twelve of the fifteen Provincial Pradesh Congress Committees nominated him. It is noteworthy that not a single Pradesh Congress Committee voted for Nehru to be the next party president or Vice President of the Viceroy's Executive Council.

Thus, these two positions and the office of the Prime Minister of India were rightfully Patel's. Nehru was undoubtedly very popular among the people, but he had been bested by Patel. It must be clarified here that it was the Congress Working Committee that voted to elect Patel, and not the larger All India Congress Committee. If the AICC or the entire Congress had voted, there's a strong possibility that Nehru, as the most popular Congress leader after Gandhi, would have won hands down. But that will have to remain in the realms of conjecture. The rules of engagement stipulated a vote in the CWC, where Patel commanded an overwhelming majority—and he won. It must also be clarified that the electorate was not voting for the first Prime Minister of Independent India. But that was the consequence of the vote.

It was Patel who, therefore, emerged as the popular choice to become the leader of free India.

But Patel had not reckoned with Gandhi, who considered Nehru, 20 years his junior, more like a son than a colleague. He perhaps felt that the Harrow and Cambridge-educated Nehru was more likely to lead India "in international affairs more effectively than Patel"; or he may have felt Nehru's greater acceptance among Muslims to be an advantage in the newly partitioned country[2]; or he may have simply allowed his own fondness for Nehru to overrule the democratic principles that had decided the contest in Patel's favour. Whatever the reason behind the Mahatma's decision, it was a costly mistake on his part to veto the will of the electorate.

But it was of a piece with Gandhi's verdicts on at least two previous occasions—in 1929 and again in 1936—when Gandhi had used his moral authority and his personal capital to push Nehru's name despite the presence of other stalwart frontrunners. His reasoning had been straightforward and simple, at least in his own mind. Explaining the rationale behind his choice in 1929, he said in a statement on August 1, 1929, that "those who know the relations that subsist between Jawaharlal and me know that his being in the chair is as good as my being in it. We may have intellectual differences but our hearts are one."[3]

Gandhi himself had been the overwhelming choice of the Congress delegates who made up the electoral college. Ten of the eighteen provincial Congress Committees wanted him to be president, five wanted Sardar Patel, and three backed Nehru. So, in effect, he was handing over his own chair to his chosen disciple. But C. Rajagopalachari, aka Rajaji, backed by Patel, was the odds-on favourite in 1936, and Patel himself was the clear choice in 1946. But such was the respect and moral authority of Gandhi that Patel and Rajaji obediently stepped aside to honour their leader's wishes.

What proved to be a disappointment for Patel and Rajaji proved to be a major setback for India's developmental goals. As subsequent events proved, Nehru's socialist policies, neglect of education and agriculture, focus on heavy industries, inadequate attention to employment generation, suspicion of trade and commerce, an elite bias and, lastly, his utter disdain for India's traditional knowledge systems and native intelligence collectively fostered what his followers proudly showcased as "modern India," but which became, in actual fact, a poster child of a poverty-stricken Third World nation with a begging bowl.

Nehru and Patel Could Not Work in Tandem

Gandhi's vision of Nehru and Patel working in tandem to lift India out of poverty and destitution proved to be stillborn. Despite the tremendous respect the two stalwarts of the freedom struggle had for each other, they fought tooth and nail over the direction independent India would take on its economy, social policies and foreign relations. However, contrary to some commentaries, they never let their ideological differences degenerate into personal attacks and took care to confine their divergent political outlooks within the norms of civility and mutual respect.

Although Nehru's biographers and later historians have tried hard to paper over the cracks in the relationship, a cursory reading of contemporary accounts and correspondence between the two from August 15, 1947 till Patel's death in 1950 shows how far the two men had pulled apart on the issues that defined them. As Ashoka Mody writes in *India Is Broken*, Nehru "seemed to buy into the rumour" that "Patel, as home minister, was protecting and aiding Hindus but not Muslims." Mody argues that "in the Indian areas marked by Hindu–Muslim tensions, the government machinery had collapsed or had become fiercely partisan."[4]

This rumour though had no basis. Mody quotes Rajmohan Gandhi, the Mahatma's grandson and Patel's biographer, as writing that Patel "was unquestionably aroused more by a report of so Hindu and Sikh deaths than by another 50 Muslim deaths, but his hand was just."[5]

Patel, on the other hand, was impatient with Nehru's soft approach towards Pakistani leaders who seemed to be paying only lip service to containing the violence against Hindus in the then newly formed state of Pakistan.

Kashmir: A Point of Disagreement

They also clashed over Kashmir. As minister in charge of integrating the erstwhile princely states into India, Patel had got down to the task with the ruthless efficiency he had come to be known for. Maharaja Hari Singh, who had avoided merging his state with either India or Pakistan, vacillated for a couple of months and then appealed to India for help when a Pakistan-backed tribal militia launched a full-scale invasion of the princely state. Patel was in charge initially but was blindsided when Nehru asserted his authority as Prime Minister to take control of India's Kashmir policy. Gandhi had to intervene to try and resolve the issues between his two principal political disciples but fell to an assassin's bullets before the growing chasm could be bridged.

This sudden cataclysmic development led to a temporary rapprochement between the two. "We have had our differences," Nehru admitted in a radio address, "but India at least should know that these differences have been overshadowed by fundamental agreements about the most important aspects of our public life." A few days later, he wrote to Patel asking them to work together as friends and colleagues.

Patel, ever gracious to his younger colleague and rival for the Mahatma's affections, replied: "I am deeply touched, indeed, overwhelmed. We have been lifelong friends and comrades in a common cause."[6]

Thus, a parting of ways between these two stalwarts of the freedom struggle, which had seemed imminent, was averted. But their differences continued to simmer, most notably on the direction of India's economy and its foreign policy choices.

Patel Was Not Keen on Socialism

Patel did not share Nehru's admiration for the policies and apparent successes of the Soviet Union. Unlike his younger colleague, he was not at all enamoured of socialism. And though he did not oppose planning per se, he was not particularly impressed by Nehru's enthusiasm for a technocrat-run Planning Commission as the centre of economic decision making in India.

Matters came to a head when a draft Congress resolution backed by Nehru called for the Planning Commission to eliminate "the motive of private gain in economic activity."[7]

The first Prime Minister of independent India had given an inkling of his thinking in his address as president of the Congress in 1936. In that seminal speech, he had said:

> I am convinced that the only key to the solution of the world's problems and of India's problems lies in socialism, and when I use this word I do so not in a vague humanitarian way but in the scientific, economic sense. Socialism is, however, something even more than an economic doctrine; it is a philosophy of life and as such also, it appeals to me. I see no way of ending the poverty, the vast unemployment, the degradation and the subjection of the Indian people except through socialism. That involves vast and revolutionary changes in our political and social structure, the ending of vested interests in land and industry, as well as the feudal and autocratic Indian States system. *That means the ending of private property, except in a restricted sense, and the replacement of the present profit system by a higher ideal of co-operative service.* It means ultimately a change in our instincts and habits and desires. In short, it means a new civilization, radically different from the present capitalist order. Some glimpse we can have of this new civilization in the territories of the U.S.S.R. Much has happened there which has pained me greatly and with which I disagree, but I look upon that great and fascinating unfolding of a new order and a new civilization as the most promising feature of our dismal age. If the future is full of hope it is largely because of Soviet Russia and what it has done, and I am convinced that, if some world catastrophe does not intervene, this new civilization will spread to other lands and put an end to the wars and conflicts which capitalism feeds.
>
> I do not know how or when this new order will come to India. I imagine that every country will fashion it after

its own way and fit it in with its national genius. But the essential basis of that order must remain and be a link in the world order that will emerge out of the present chaos.

Socialism is thus for me not merely an economic doctrine which I favour; it is a vital creed which I hold with all my head and heart. I work for Indian independence because the nationalist in me cannot tolerate alien domination; I work for it even more because for me it is the inevitable step to social and economic change. I should like the Congress to become a socialist organization and to join hands with the other forces in the world who are working for the new civilization. But I realise that the majority in the Congress, as it is constituted to-day, may not be prepared to go thus far. We are a nationalist organization and we think and work on the nationalist plane. It is evident enough now that this is too narrow even for the limited objective of political independence, and so we talk of the masses and their economic needs. But still most of us hesitate, because of our nationalist backgrounds, to take a step which might frighten away some vested interests. Most of those interests are already ranged against us and we can expect little from them except opposition even in the political struggle.

Much as I wish for the advancement of socialism in this country, I have no desire to force the issue in the Congress and thereby create difficulties in the way of our struggle for independence. I shall co-operate gladly and with all the strength in me with all those who work for independence even though they do not agree with the socialist solution. But I shall do so stating my position frankly and hoping in course of time to convert the Congress and the country to it, for only thus can I see it achieving independence. It should surely be possible for all of us who believe in independence to join our ranks together even though we

> might differ on the social issue. The Congress has been in the past a broad front representing various opinions joined together by that common bond. It must continue as such even though the difference of those opinions becomes more marked.[8]

Mark the words he used. "I see no way of ending the poverty, the vast unemployment, the degradation and the subjection of the Indian people except through socialism… That means the ending of private property, except in a restricted sense, and the replacement of the present profit system by a higher ideal of co-operative service… It means a new civilization, radically different from the present capitalist order."

This clearly showed the mind of an already converted individual, convinced about the ideological dogma he had come to hold dear. Nehru was, obviously, not willing to consider that there could be other paths to development and social and economic uplift open to India that could avoid the gross humanitarian tragedy that had come to befall the people of the Soviet Union under Stalin. It did not matter when he was merely the Congress president and a leader of the freedom movement. At best, it was the statement of intent of an individual. The Mahatma had then ensured that Nehru's leftwing idiom did not seep into the Congress resolution and that the party remained a centrist political organisation.

In his autobiography too, he had clearly exposed his bias against business:

> Right through history, the old Indian idea did not glorify political and economic triumph and it looked down upon money and the professional money-lending class. Today, it (the older culture) is fighting against a new and all-

powerful opposition from the *bania* civilization of the capitalist West.[9]

The Basis of Nehru's Bias

Nehru's prejudice had its intellectual basis in his education at the elite Harrow and Cambridge University, where he came to acquire the British upper class aversion to trade and industry. He also came under the influence of the Fabians during this phase of his life.

As Prime Minister of India, as the mover and shaker whose decisions and opinions impacted the lives and the futures of hundreds of millions of his people, he was in a position to implement his disruptive and economically disastrous ideas. There was no Gandhi to rein him in.

Congress Elections Became a Proxy Battle That Nehru Lost

The rank and file of the Congress was still not totally convinced that Nehru's socialist vision was the only path to India's redemption. This became starkly evident in the Congress presidential elections that followed in 1950. The two candidates were Purushottam Das Tandon and Acharya Jivatram Bhagwandas Kripalani. Tandon, who had unsuccessfully contested for the post against outgoing party president Bhogaraju Pattabhi Sitaramayya in the previous round of elections, and Kripalani, who had taken over as Congress chief from Nehru in September 1947, were backed by Patel and Nehru, respectively, in their proxy battle for control of the party and government.

Tandon won the election, proving once again that Patel's iron grip over the party was intact. But this was to be his last hurray. Three months later, Patel suffered a massive heart attack at Birla House in Bombay and passed away on the morning of December 15, 1950. The relationship between Tandon as party president and Nehru as Prime Minister, fractious at the best of times, soon reached a breaking point. With Patel no longer around to back him, and in the face of opposition from the Nehru camp, Tandon's position became increasingly untenable, and he resigned in September 1951.

Nehru Centralises Power in Himself

Rather than risk another independent-minded candidate, Nehru decided that it would be safer to take up the position of party chief himself. As the last surviving member of the "big three" Congress leaders (Gandhi, Patel and Nehru), he was elected the president of the Congress for the next two terms, after which he ensured that the position went to trusted colleagues only.[10]

Thus, the system of checks and balances that kept the Prime Minister's powers in check came to be dismantled. With Patel dead and his followers orphaned, the bulwark against the socialist onslaught on India's economic future disappeared. India's thin sliver of middle class and the vast masses of poor would have to grapple with socialist sloth, inefficiency, shortages, poverty, homelessness, hunger, black marketing, crony capitalism and corruption over the next four decades even as India's ruling classes offered only socialist rhetoric as a balm for the economic hardships that confronted the young nation.

What If…

A counterfactual question that keeps surfacing is: what if Patel had become the first Prime Minister of independent India instead of Nehru? Would India have looked significantly different from what it is today?

Much as Patel fans and Nehru detractors might like to imagine, the truth is we do not know and cannot tell with any degree of certitude. That's because Patel died in 1950. That is a historical fact that cannot be altered. So, Nehru would almost certainly have become Prime Minister after that. All the economic missteps that hobbled India's growth for decades were initiated after that. It is not certain that any systems that Patel put in place to keep Nehru's socialist zeal in check would have remained standing after his passing.

Perhaps the only crisis that could have been averted was the one over Kashmir. If Patel had been at the helm from 1947–50, it is almost certain that India would not have halted military operations and gone to the United Nations. It is also likely that Patel as Prime Minister would not have countenanced the insertion of Article 370 into India's Constitution. However, the equally damaging Article 35A came into the statute books in 1954, i.e. after Patel's demise. Though Nehru would have been heading the government then, it is uncertain if this statute would have come into existence in the absence of Article 370.

The Balochistan Miss

Kalat, which is now a district in the province of Balochistan, was a princely state with a complex relationship with British India. Mir Ahmadyar Khan, the Khan of Kalat, as its hereditary ruler was called, did not initially want to accede to Pakistan and even declared independence on August 12, 1947. But Pakistani leader Mohammad Ali Jinnah wanted it in Pakistan and began to exert military pressure to merge it with Pakistan.

After considering his options, the Khan of Kalat expressed his desire to accede to India. But he was shocked to hear V.P. Menon, India's Secretary in the Ministry of States, who was helping Sardar Patel integrate princely states into India, tell All India Radio on March 27, 1948, that "the Khan of Kalat was pressing India to accept Kalat's accession," but add that "India would have nothing to do with it."[11] It is believed that Patel was blindsided by this comment and the next day dialled back from this position and refuted this statement, but it was too late.

Jinnah was waiting for just this opening. He ordered his military to march into Kalat the next day and forced the Khan to accede to Pakistan. Kalat was merged with the surrounding areas and became part of Balochistan.

So, it is possible that if Patel had been Prime Minister in that era, Kalat and possibly other parts of Balochistan could have been parts of India.

So, if the Mahatma had not intervened on behalf of Nehru in 1946, India could have been spared 70 years of trauma and the resulting bloodshed in Kashmir and could have been holding a strategic ace to the west of Pakistan.

Rajaji Opposes Socialism

Chakravarty Rajagopalachari, better known as Rajaji, was another stalwart of the freedom movement who enjoyed great respect among the Indian people. A renowned Hindu scholar, his translations of the Bhagwat Gita, Ramayan and Mahabharat were popular among educated Hindus. His stature led to him to being appointed the last Governor General of India.

He was vehemently opposed to Nehru's tilt towards socialism. A firm believer in the free market, he believed that newly independent India "needed as much competition as possible and as much planning as necessary." He and his followers were also resolutely opposed to Nehru's five-year plans, which led to severe foreign exchange shortages, large shortfalls in employment generation, and also unreasonable restraints on the private sector.

Unfortunately for India, Rajaji only had the intellectual heft and the respect of India's thin sliver of middle class behind him but not the political support needed to force the government to change course. The vast majority of Indians continued to remain in thrall of Nehru's socialist rhetoric despite its abject failure to deliver on its promises. When Rajaji formed his Swatantra Party in 1959, it did well only in some pockets in the next general elections in 1962 but could not challenge the dominance of the Congress across large swathes of India. It shone brightly on India's political firmament for a few years before vanishing into oblivion.

The challenge before the government of India was to find an ideal path to transition from a state of underdevelopment, illiteracy and economic backwardness to a stage of rapid economic growth. Despite lots of rhetoric about selecting a mixed economy model of development, which, theoretically, would draw on the best practices from the socialist and free market models, India's economic planners displayed a marked preference for the state-led model of development that empowered a small clique of bureaucrats and politicians and snuffed the life out of Indian entrepreneurship. Nehru's insistence on ushering in a "socialist pattern of society"—and his complete command over the government and the party following Patel's demise—led the country into a *cul de sac* from which it began to emerge four decades later when confronted with imminent bankruptcy and the abject failure of the Soviet model on which it was based.

As a result, India missed the bus on the unprecedented global expansion of trade and prosperity that rebuilt Western Europe and Japan into the economic powerhouses they had been before World War II and enabled countries in East and Southeast Asia to leapfrog ahead of India on all social and economic indicators. The governance lapses and the missed opportunities on the economic front—which have not received as much attention as other policy initiatives such as Nehru's foreign policy blunders, the missteps in Kashmir and the appeasement of minorities—created the triple-headed monsters of corruption, nepotism and inefficiency, which engulfed Indian society like a cancer in the decades during and following his rule.

The Balance Sheet Approach

Nehru and his successors undoubtedly had some great achievements to their credit. It was audacious and far-sighted of Nehru, as the leader of a poor, "Third World" nation, to set up the IITs, the IIMs, the Indian Space Research Organisation, and the infrastructure for atomic research.

Lal Bahadur Shastri initiated the Green Revolution, which made India self-sufficient in foodgrains. Indira Gandhi launched the White Revolution, which transformed India into a milk-surplus nation. She also led India brilliantly in the lead-up to the 1971 war with Pakistan by signing the Peace and Friendship Treaty with the Soviet Union to keep the US at bay, and created the conditions that gave birth to Bangladesh. That was undoubtedly her finest hour. She also made India a nuclear power by testing the N-bomb at the Pokhran test range on May 18, 1974.

Her son and successor, Rajiv Gandhi, set off the IT and telecom revolutions that have served India so well and helped transform the country into the world's back office.

These are not achievements that can be ignored, and the leaders who were responsible must be given due credit.

If one were to draw a balance sheet of the first 44 years of India's development journey as an independent nation, these achievements would embellish its asset side.

The historians who recorded that era forgot, perhaps deliberately, that every balance sheet also has a liability side. We were taught—actually, indoctrinated with—only the entries on the asset side of the country's balance sheet to paint the rulers as great visionaries who were the architects and builders of a strong, resilient and modern India. That will undoubtedly be the conclusion if one studies only the positive side of the balance sheet.

The liability side, which has been whitewashed out of the narrative, changes the picture completely. Nehruvian naïveté cost India one-third of Kashmir and 77 years of bloodshed and national trauma. It cost us a chance to include Balochistan, Gwadar, Nepal and Coco Islands in our republic. His inexplicable fascination with China denied India a seat on the United Nations Security Council. Then, he signed a completely one-sided Indus Waters Treaty that handed over 80 percent of the waters to the lower riparian state in a misconceived and misguided spirit of goodwill towards Pakistan.

On the social and economic fronts, his elitist education policy kept hundreds of millions of Indians over three generations illiterate, destitute and without hope, and his illogical focus on capital-intensive heavy industries kept adding millions to the army of unemployed people as every Plan fell short of achieving its employment target. His ideological aversion to foreign trade kept India insular and prevented the country from benefitting from the growing global trade that lifted countries in East and South East Asia out of poverty and into the ranks of middle-income countries.

Then, the License Permit Raj institutionalised corruption and crony capitalism, which reached new heights under his daughter, Indira Gandhi.

Her long rule did not have any significant economic achievements except the White Revolution. Little wonder, then, that apart from the 1971 War, her rule is mainly remembered for the imposition of Emergency.

And Rajiv Gandhi's rule immediately brings to mind the massacre of Sikhs in the aftermath of Indira Gandhi's assassination, scandals like Bofors and how Union Carbide Chairman Warren Anderson was escorted out of India, the law to overturn the Shah Bano judgment, and the draconian defamation Bill, which was a naked attempt to censor the press—in keeping with his family's tradition going back to the First Amendment and the Emergency.

The history we were taught and the public discourse—dominated by the Marxist intellectual aristocracy allied to the ruling dynasty of the time—did not ask the following questions:

- Why did India have the world's largest number of illiterate people in 1991 (the end of the period under review in this book)?
- Why did independent India not reform the bureaucracy, and why did it continue with the colonial era system of governance?
- Why did the backlog of unemployment keep rising every year till 1991?
- Why did India need to survive on PL480 wheat shipments from the US until the late 1960s?
- Why were there shortages of and a black market in almost every item till 1991?
- Who was responsible for the Nehruvian rate of growth, which was dubbed "Hindu rate of growth" by its authors to shift the blame for the lack of growth to the victims?
- Why did the Indian Prime Ministers have to go around the world with a begging bowl?
- Why was India on the brink of bankruptcy in 1991?
- Why did the country have to endure de facto censorship throughout the period under review?
- Where did we go wrong? And who is responsible for this?

Of the 44 years between 1947 and 1991, the Nehru–Gandhi family ruled India directly for 38 years (Nehru's 17 years +

Indira Gandhi's 16 years + Rajiv Gandhi's 5 years). And the Nehruvian policies were followed throughout that period.

A fair and honest answer to these questions would have burst the balloon of Nehruvian success and debunked the myth about the First Family of the Congress being the architect of a strong and resilient modern India.

Instead, the Nehru–Gandhi family's years of direct rule would surely rank as the greatest betrayal in the history of democracy—where one family continued to promise the moon to three generations of gullible, illiterate, trusting and unexposed Indians, and fed them with rhetoric and empty promises only to secure the throne for itself.

But surely, some people must have benefitted from the system put in place by the first Prime Minister and followed in word and spirit by his successors till 1991.

Of course! The biggest beneficiaries were the big industrialists, the bureaucrats, the power brokers, the middlemen, the black marketeers, the Congress politicians, and a thin sliver of the middle class.

But, for the vast majority, their rule was a disaster that left more than 50 percent of Indians illiterate, unemployed, hungry, destitute, and bereft of any hope of a better tomorrow.

Ironically, it took the first Congress Prime Minister from outside the Nehru–Gandhi family to dig India out of the deep hole his predecessors had dug for the country and to set it on the path of development and upward mobility.

A fair appraisal of the period would show the liability side of India's balance sheet in its first forty-four years as an independent nation to be much heavier than its asset side.

2

Missing the Bus

Independence had brought in its wake the largest exchange of population in the history of mankind, unprecedented human suffering, dismemberment of a country, and disruption of organic trade ties between the provinces that opted to become Pakistan and those that remained within India. The Indian economy was classified as underdeveloped. Two centuries of British colonial exploitation had left it with low per capita income, low national income, poor levels of education, low life expectancy, and widespread poverty.

The challenges before the new government were immense. There were no precedents of any colonised nation embarking on a journey of development that India's leaders could use as a template. An influential section within the Congress party led by Jawaharlal Nehru wanted to set India on the path of socialism, even though most such demands stopped well short of the dictatorial and ruthless methods employed in the Soviet Union. Another section of the party led by Sardar Vallabhbhai Patel preferred the tried and test free market model that had served much of the world well over the previous two centuries.

But even as India's two leading politicians were shadow boxing over the direction of the newly independent country's economy, the world was undergoing an unprecedented economic expansion, opening up massive growth opportunities

Most studies and analyses have focused disproportionately on the problems India faced at the time and the challenges it had to overcome. There can be no denying that these were of Himalayan proportions. But equally true was the fact that the external environment offered an unprecedented opportunity to leapfrog several generations of development in only a few years.

Golden Age of Capitalism

At that time, India was standing at an inflexion point. It could have clambered up the development ladder and improved the lives and livelihoods of 33 crore human beings—one-sixth of mankind—or it could have fumbled and faltered, as it did, and, thus, condemned its people to at least two or three generations more of destitution and distress.

The post-World War II economic boom, which came to be dubbed the Golden Age of Capitalism, brought unprecedented prosperity, sustained growth and full employment in the United States, the Soviet Union, Western Europe, East Asia and Southeast Asia. Countries like the United Kingdom, France, West Germany, Belgium, Austria, Japan and Greece, which had been reduced to rubble during the World War rose again from the ashes of destruction like the Phoenix of Greek mythology.

Economist Roger Middleton and economic historian Robert Skidelsky have set 1950 and 1951, respectively, as the start of this boom. This period of economic expansion ended with the oil shock of 1973, though some other estimates place its end in 1970. Countries belonging to the Organisation for Economic Cooperation and Development (OECD) grew at an average of 4 percent per annum during the 1950s and 5 percent in the decade that followed as post-War reconstruction helped create a new consumerism that engulfed much of the world. Japan and Germany took advantage of this global economic boom to race ahead of the UK in overall GDP, while Britain itself was experiencing the greatest absolute prosperity in its history. In Asia, countries like South Korea, Taiwan, Hong Kong and Singapore, which joined the development race late, also leapfrogged ahead of India, growing at a very high—often double-digit—rates through the 1960s and early 1970s.

British Prime Minister Harod Macmillan said in a speech in 1957:

> Let us be frank about it. Most of our people have never had it so good. Go round the country, go to the industrial towns, go to the farms and you will see a state of prosperity such as we have never had in my lifetime—nor indeed in the history of this country.[12]

Enormous amounts of wealth were being created in almost every country that cared to participate in this boom. In the two decades between 1948 and 1968, the total volume of merchandise exports grew an incredible 290 percent and the expansion of trade far exceeded the growth in output.

It needed sagacity, an open mind, a spirit of experimentation to see what worked, visionary leadership, and a shedding of ideological blinkers to benefit from this global economic boom. India was crying out for a visionary leader who could seize the opportunity and propel the country forward—like Lee Kuan Yew in Singapore a decade-and-a-half later and Deng Xiaoping in China 15 years after that. Unfortunately for Indian citizens, India's top political leadership failed to get rid of the socialist blinkers that coloured its views. So, India continued to languish among the ranks of Third World countries even as its neighbours in Asia—most notably Japan, South Korea, Taiwan, Singapore, Hong Kong, Indonesia, Malaysia, and Thailand—forged ahead on almost every economic and social indicators. When ordinary humans err, it is only their families and friends who suffer; but when big leaders make mistakes, millions of people—and generations that follow—continue to pay a heavy price for decades.

This is all the more tragic because Prime Minister Nehru was an economic moderniser with a scientific temper, who believed that rapid industrialisation was the path to economic and social emancipation for the Indian people. This was in stark contrast to the quaint Gandhian concept of encouraging micro-scale village and home industries as the way to uplift the Indian masses. He had the global exposure, close personal connections with some of the leading economic and political thinkers of his time, and the political heft to carry the Indian people along with him. It was sheer tragedy that he chose to be guided by his ideology and his instincts rather than by the evidence around him that was growing in volume with each passing day.

The Bombay Plan

To be fair to Nehru, he was not the only one in thrall of state intervention in the Indian economy. During the War, a group of eight leading Indian industrialists—J.R.D. Tata. G.D. Birla, Lala Shri Ram, Katurbhai Lalbhai, Purushottamdas Thakurdas, A.D. Shroff, Sir Ardeshir Dalal and John

Mathai—drew up a blueprint for industrialisation of post-Independence India titled *A Brief Memorandum Outlining a Plan of Economic Development for India*. Popularly called the Bombay Plan, the first part was published in 1944, and the second part the following year. The stated goals of the plan were to double the country's agricultural output and lay the foundation for a five-fold expansion of the industrial sector. The overall investment figure was envisaged at Rs 100 billion over a period of 15 years.

A basic assumption of the Bombay Plan was that Indian industry would not be able to compete in a free market economy. It, therefore, called for government intervention in and strict regulation of industrial activity to protect Indian industry from foreign companies and accepted the circumscribing of rights attached to private property.

The Bombay Plan also proposed:

- deficit financing, if necessary, to usher in equitable growth
- the setting up of a public sector to incubate the establishment of critical industries
- planned purchases by the government and the public sector of goods produced by the private sector, and
- a transition from an agricultural society to an industrialised one.

The rationale for leading industrialists supporting Nehru's ideas on central planning will have to remain in the realm of conjecture. The most charitable explanation is that they were convinced that the market was not sufficiently developed in

India to fuel rapid growth and development. But it cannot be denied that they had gained tremendously from the high tariffs imposed in the inter-war years that had protected them from cheaper imports. Quite naturally, they wanted the status quo to continue.

The industrialists did not advocate a total ban on foreign capital and technology. They, however, wanted foreign debt and loans instead of equity investments by foreign players and that too under strict state control. They also wanted a complete ban on foreign investments in areas like banking, insurance and aviation, and nationalisation where such investment existed. It should be noted that the Tata Group then owned India's only airline and the Birlas ran businesses in the banking and insurance sectors. So, it was natural for them to try and preclude foreign competition on their turfs.

Quite astonishingly, the plan recommended state control and limits on the private sector and even accepted restrictions on rights attached to private property as well as state control and oversight in areas such as price control, dividend distribution, foreign trade and foreign exchange. It also advocated licensing production, the allocation of capital goods, and the distribution and sale of consumer goods.

The words "socialist" and "socialism" were not mentioned, but the similarities between the Bombay Plan and the subsequent policy measures unveiled by the Nehru government in its quest to usher in a socialist pattern of society are difficult to miss. Though the precise details of India's planning documents differed, their profiles are surprisingly similar.

Independent India had inherited a system of rationing, price controls and bureaucratic oversight that had been put in place during the closing stages of the British Raj and the Second World War. These were lapped up by politicians and bureaucrats to perpetuate their control over the business and industrial sector. Other countries that had put in place similar restrictions on their private sector began to dismantle them after the war. But in India, they not only continued but were strengthened and expanded, with disastrous consequences for the economy.

Prime Minister Nehru's socialist zeal became evident—and, indeed, became a shield for the sloth and corruption that engulfed the public sector—when he, on more than one occasion, defended the losses incurred by public sector companies, saying their job was not to make profits but to achieve social objectives.

In his book *The Dynasty*, retired IAS officer S.S. Gill writes:

> At least in the earlier stages, it was widely believed that public sector was not expected to make profits. This mindset promoted a style of management where some nebulous notions of social good obscured the importance of generating surpluses for reinvestment.[13]

As a consequence, India's large public sector units soon degenerated into the personal fiefdoms of powerful politicians and bureaucrats, effectively making public assets the private property of a privileged few. And government regulation of industry soon became a mechanism for rent seeking by ruling party politicians and crony capitalism by a coterie of industrialists close to the establishment.

The Birth of License Permit Raj

In what is arguably the first major "socialist" intervention in the Indian economy, the Nehru government passed a bizarre and regressive law called the Industries (Development and Regulation) Act 1951, which contributed significantly to setting back India's journey to economic freedom by at least four decades. It was only in 1991 that Prime Minister P.V. Narasimha Rao abolished licenses for most industries and freed Indian industry from the shackles that had hobbled its growth and kept the country poor since Independence.

The objectives of the Act were to

- enable the central government to implement its industrial policy as approved by the Parliament
- bring under central control the development and regulation of industries that were considered of national importance
- ensure planning of future development along balanced lines of industries across the country
- maintain regional balance in industrial development
- prevent monopolies and concentration of wealth in a few hands
- protect small scale industries

Although the goals were laudable, the law effectively tied up Indian industry in excessive regulations, red tape and bureaucracy. Even small capacity expansions as well as new projects needed to be vetted through a lengthy approval process that encouraged both inefficiency and massive opportunities for rent seeking.

The Act's licensing requirements, including the need for government approvals for capacity expansion and new projects, have been criticised for creating lengthy bureaucratic processes, leading to delays, and discouraging entrepreneurship. The entire process was not only time-consuming but also completely opaque and non-transparent and created massive room for arbitrary, non-merit decision-making, which was fully exploited by politicians, bureaucrats, industrialists and power brokers to kill the spirit of innovation and entrepreneurship of all but the most intrepid or the best connected. How this worked is described more fully in the following section on crony capitalism. This made it almost impossible for new entrants to disrupt the market with innovations and new products, technologies and business models.

The scope of the First Schedule of the Act, which lists the industries to be regulated, included even small-scale industries, thus, effectively blocking a route for many potential entrepreneurs to bring new products and innovations to Indian industry. This severely impacted the growth and competitiveness of the SME sector and killed potential avenues for rapid employment generation.

Industrial Policy Resolution 1956

In 1956, the Nehruvian establishment brought in more regulations, which further fettered growth, innovation and entrepreneurship. The Industrial Policy Resolution effectively became the economic constitution of the country for the next 35 years. Very few deviations from its stifling controls were permitted, and many were made more stringent and draconian, leading to more opportunities for bribery, corruption and crony capitalism.

It was adopted by Parliament in April 1956, and the stated purpose of the policy was to help establish a "socialist pattern of society"; it increased the powers of the government to regulate and restrict Indian industry.

It had three schedules that laid out which industries would remain the exclusive preserve of the public sector, which industries would allow limited private sector entrepreneurship, and which would be fully open to the private sector.

Schedule A listed the following industries, which were reserved exclusively for the public sector: atomic energy; minerals specified in the schedule to the Atomic Energy (Control of Production and Use) Order, 1953; iron and steel; coal and lignite; mineral oils; mining of iron ore; manganese ore; chrome-ore; gypsum; sulphur; gold and diamonds; mining and processing of copper; lead; zinc; tin; molybdenum and wolfram; arms and ammunitions; heavy castings and forgings of iron and steel; heavy plant and machinery for core industries; heavy electrical plants and large hydraulic and steam turbines; aircraft; air transport; railways; ship building; telecom; and electricity generation and distribution.

Schedule B listed industries that would over time come under the ownership and control of the state and in which all new industries would be set up in the public sector. However, the private sector would be allowed to play a supplementary role to support the efforts of the government.

Schedule C contained all the remaining industries that would be left to the private sector subject to stifling state controls.

The 1951 Act and the 1956 policy, thus, constituted the bedrock of the industrial development doctrine of the Nehru government and all subsequent governments till 1991. These and the Five-Year Plans were in keeping with the Soviet model of development of which Nehru continued to remain in thrall despite the revelation—around the same time as the passage of the 1956 policy by the Indian Parliament—that Stalin's alleged success at industrialising the USSR had come at a huge human cost and on the back of the largest genocide in the history of mankind (till it was overtaken in scale by Mao's serial genocides in China).

Nehru was too intelligent, well-informed and erudite a person not to have noticed the huge caveats that came with the Stalinist model, but he was too blinded by ideology to take note and perhaps also too egoistic to admit that he had been wrong. So, his government refused to change course, and India continued its slow but steady march towards bankruptcy three-and-a-half decades later.

However, if one analyses the facts dispassionately, it will be evident that it was India's leading industrialists who had authored the plan that planted the seeds of licensing in India. By advocating for a strict ban on foreign equity investments in Indian industry, restrictions on expansion of capacity, imposition of price controls and restrictions on imports, the Bombay Plan and the subsequent policy thrust of the Indian government were tailormade blueprints for perpetuating the oligopolies that dominated the Indian business firmament of the 1940s and 1950s. Industrialists would obviously support a system that guaranteed a closed market devoid of any meaningful competition, opportunities for supernormal profits, and a continuation of their hegemony and dominance over the Indian business environment.

The politicians and bureaucrats, obviously, must have welcomed the opportunity for rent-seeking and corruption that soon became an all-pervasive cancer eating away at the sinews and innards of the Indian economy and, indeed, every walk of life.

What is surprising is that Nehru did not notice this or, if he did, why he took no steps to prevent this.

Crony Capitalism and Systemic Corruption

The term crony capitalism has gained great currency in recent times as a result of a political leader, a descendant of the first Prime Minister, accusing the ruling dispensation and two large business houses of indulging in it. The delicious irony is that the system he has been ranting against was put in place by governments headed by his ancestors and run by the party he belongs to.

As Gurcharan Das describes so eloquently in his book *India Unbound*:

> An untrained army of underpaid, third-rate engineers at the Directorate General of Technical Development, operating on the basis of inadequate and ill-organized information and without clear cut criteria, vetted thousands of applications on an ad hoc basis. The low-level functionaries took months in the futile micro-view of an application and finally sent it for approval to the administrative ministry. The ministry again lost months

> reviewing the same data before it sent the application to an interministerial licensing committee of senior bureaucrats, who were equally ignorant of entrepreneurial realities, and who also operated on ad hoc criteria in the absence of well-ordered priorities. Once it cleared the licensing committee, it was sent to the minister for final approval.[14]

This long and tortuous journey, which often took several years, in no way signalled the end of the entrepreneur's travails. That is because

> the investor had to seek approval for the import of machinery from the capital goods licensing committee. If a foreign collaboration was involved, an interministerial foreign agreement committee also had to give its consent. If finance was needed from a state financial institution, the same scrutiny had to be repeated afresh. The result was enormous delays, sometimes lasting years, with staggering opportunities for corruption. By the time the backbreaking process of moving files from office to office was completed, many an entrepreneur had lost heart.[15]

The entire architecture of the scheme was tailormade for rent seeking, corruption and sleaze, and that is what it resulted in. Every large business house in the country set up huge "liaison offices" in the national capital manned by executives whose only job was to monitor, expedite and, in some cases, block the movement of files, documents and information in and from government offices. It led to a situation where the same business house would apply for licenses under a number of different names and, having got the coveted permission to start business under more than one company, would sit on some of them. This "hoarding" of licensed capacity would substantially foreclose competition and often resulted in monopolies, duopolies or oligopolies that led to shortages of the given product or commodity. This, in turn, bred a black market for almost every conceivable product, including cars, scooters, motorcycles, cooking oils, baby foods, etc.

If an enterprising entrepreneur saw an opportunity in the shortages and increased production to meet the unmet demand, he would be in big trouble. That is because it was against the law to manufacture beyond the licensed capacity and doing so could land the industrialist in jail. It was an irony to beat all ironies. A country plagued by shortages of almost every item had laws to jail business leaders who walked the extra mile to mitigate the scarcity. Unsurprisingly, India was the only country in the world with such an absurd law.

Most industrialists did not dare protest these restrictive laws. But Rahul Bajaj did at a Monopolies Commission hearing. The judge asked him why he had produced scooters well beyond his licensed capacity. In reply, he bravely answered, "Sir, my grandfather went to jail for my country's freedom. I stand ready to do the same on behalf of my motherland." The government quietly dropped the case.[16]

B.K. Nehru, the Prime Minister's cousin, a senior bureaucrat of the time and Indian ambassador to the US, criticised this in his autobiography. "With the benefit of hindsight, it seems totally absurd that a country wanting to develop its industry should prescribe for its establishment conditions that were guaranteed to strangle it." He went on to lament that few people in government had any idea how industry ought to be run.[17]

Nehru, who, like his advisors, had zero experience in running industries, was ideologically committed to ensuring that the public sector should remain at the commanding heights of the economy. With little appetite for getting into the minutiae of governance, he left it to his untrained-for-business bureaucrats and advisors to run the economy. Not unexpectedly, their interventions led the Indian economy into a quagmire in a very short time.

C. Rajagopalachari, who vehemently opposed regulations to stifle industry, coined the term "License Permit Raj," which was a play on the oppressive British Raj. His fears that it would lead to unbridled corruption and economic stagnation proved prescient, but no one in power heeded his warnings when he first sounded the alarm.

The subliminal message being sent to industry at large was blunt: learn to profit from shortages; do not display much entrepreneurial flair; and play by the unwritten rules of the game—all the while paying homage to the establishment.

Within a decade of winning political independence, India's political establishment had put in place a system that ensured that generations of Indians would continue to eke out a miserable existence mired in poverty and hunger and unfulfilled desire.

Heavy Industries: The Miracle That Failed to Deliver

Nehru was a man in a hurry and he saw heavy industries as the vehicle that would deliver the results he was looking for. The Second Five Year Plan (1956–61) stressed rapid industrialisation, the development of the public sector and the growth of heavy industries. "The time has come to advance rapidly on the industrial front," Nehru said, and asserted that this meant "the development of heavy industries which would lay the foundations for future growth."[18]

Economist Ashok Mody speculates that Nehru was influenced by economist Paul Rosenstein Rodan's Big Push Theory. According to this theory, large-scale and coordinated investment in capital-intensive industries such as steel mills, power plants, automobile factories, large dams, entire new cities and the like would create demand for hundreds of feeder industries and set off a virtuous cycle of investment, growth and development, which would enable relatively backward countries to leapfrog up the development ladder and catch up with the developed countries. This is similar to the trickle-down theory that gained prominence later, but it was a risky gamble. At best, it promised to create jobs after a generation. If the gamble did not pay off, as it indeed did not in India's case, it would condemn three hundred million Indians—and many hundreds of millions of more people in the coming generations—to lives of penury and despair.

A visionary and a prudent man would have paused to ponder over the consequences of his decision. But Nehru and his advisors were so enamoured of the Soviet model that they ignored all the well-meaning warnings that red flagged the pitfalls of front-loading highly capital-intensive heavy industry into India's development agenda at a time when capital was scarce. Nehru said in a speech in 1956:

> Previously people's idea of industrialisation was one of increasing the output of consumer goods, with consequent employment. The idea now is ... we must start from the

> heavy, basic, mother industries. ... We must start with the production of iron and steel on a large scale. We must start with the production of the machine which makes the machine.[19]

Earlier, in 1953, he had said much the same thing:

> One thing is clear to me that if we do not develop heavy industry here then we either eliminate all modern things such as railways, airplanes and guns, ... or else import them. But to import them from abroad is to be slaves of foreign countries.[20]

He expressed these views in numerous speeches throughout his tenure as Prime Minister.

The World Bank warned in a report that while India needed steel plants, cement factories and power stations, the scale of its ambitions were out of proportion to its technical and financial capabilities. It suggested that India would be better served by producing less complex goods with more labour-intensive techniques.

Writing in the *Times of India*, Columbia University professor and former Deputy Chairman of NITI Aayog Arvind Panagariya said of Nehru's focus on heavy industries:

> The strategy brought with it many unintended consequences. All available capital was reserved for heavy industry. Given the meagre amount of capital, the scale of production in each product line within heavy industry still remained suboptimal. In parallel, light manufactures were relegated to household and small enterprises where they too remained subject to production at suboptimal scale. With higher inflation at home than abroad and a fixed exchange rate, most products soon became uncompetitive

> against their foreign counterparts and had to be protected through strict import licensing.[21]

A few years earlier, Brazil had embarked on a similar journey of rapid industrialisation and fallen on its face. In July 1954, the World Bank wrote that this development model had given Brazil "a severe crisis of industrial indigestion,"[22] leading to persistent inflation, wasted investment and a frittering away of scarce foreign exchange reserves. Nehru must have known of this, but did not learn any lessons from Brazil's example.

In 1955, shortly before the Second Plan was due to kick off, the Reserve Bank of India (RBI) warned that the Plan would cause "serious inflationary pressure."[23] It also warned about the size of the investment programme, expressing doubts over whether India had the capacity to implement and absorb such a large infusion of funds.

Instead of taking note and pausing to rethink, the Nehru–Mahalanobis duo went ahead with their Plan. (P.C. Mahalanobis was the central figure of the Second Plan). Not unsurprisingly, the strategy failed spectacularly to deliver results. Within a year of unveiling the Second Five Year Plan, India's foreign exchange reserves plummeted from $1.9 billion to $1.4 billion, a precarious drop of half a billion dollars as India's public sector companies entered into multi-year agreements for imports of equipment and technology to meet the ambitious targets of steel and coal production and for the expansion of the railways and India's power network. The multi-year agreements, entered into by some companies, meant that the demand for foreign exchange would remain high, and, as a result, India's foreign exchange reserves would continue to remain under pressure.

Important voices within the government warned the Prime Minister that his plans were not panning out as planned. Planning Minister Gulzarilal Nanda warned that the Second Plan would fall substantially short of generating the employment its authors had budgeted for. But the Prime Minister by this time was too cut off from ground realities to heed these voices of caution. Far from being a visionary who could blaze a new trail for others to follow, he was, in fact, hostage to the dominant political-economic theory of his times. And therein lay India's tragedy.

The Alternative: Wage Goods Model

Among the early naysayers in India was the classical liberal economist Bellikoth Ragunath Shenoy. Appointed in 1955 to the panel of economists to advise on the Second Five Year Plan, he submitted a famous dissent note that was, tragically but expectedly, given the zeitgeist, ignored. He warned that India did not have the means to finance such an ambitious plan and lacked the capacity to consume all that was planned to be produced. He also cautioned that the Plan's envisaged dependence on deficit financing would be inflationary and that the growing role of government in business would lead to corruption and eventually an undermining of democracy.

Two other economists, C.N. Vakil and P.R. Brahmananda, also predicted that the Plan, which largely ignored what they called "wage goods"—food, textiles and the like—would result in inflationary pressures as money incomes rose in the economy. They published their critique in a 1956 book titled *Planning for an Expanding Economy*, in which they criticised the Second Five Year Plan's focus on capital goods and heavy industries. They cautioned that the Plan would lead to inequitable development and result in limited investments in other critical sectors as a result of the scarcity of capital. They proposed an alternative model to the Nehru–Mahalanobis consensus that is known as the Wage Goods Model.

Instead of focusing on heavy industries, as the Second Five Year Plan did, they suggested that the government should prioritise the production and supply of wage goods, which they defined as goods and services such as food grains, milk and milk products, fish, eggs, meat, salt, sugar, soaps, medicines, and also essential needs like basic education, healthcare facilities and electricity. Such a strategy, they theorised, would close and then eliminate the demand–supply gap for these goods and create the right conditions for the removal of poverty and unemployment.

Their effort failed to sway the panel of economists that had been mandated to review the Plan. As many as twenty of its twenty-one members approved Mahalanobis's magnum opus, and the logic behind it came to be hardwired into Indian economic policy thinking for the next thirty-five years. Even today, despite reams of evidence to prove how the heavy industries strategy set India's development journey back by decades, influential sections of Indian academia and its intellectual establishment continue to extol the non-existent virtues of the Second Five Year Plan. Vakil and Brahmananda were thereafter kept away from all meetings related to planning. "Anyone who attacked the Mahalanobis model at that time was condemned as an anti-national or worse a CIA agent," Brahmananda later said.[24]

So convinced was Nehru about the development consensus of that era—which was that the government should take the lead in industrialisation and that heavy industries was the holy grail of development—that he refused to consider any other approach. Noted economist Dr Niranjan Rajadhyaksha wrote in the *Mint*:

> The early success of the Soviet experiment had, unfortunately, enchanted many intellectuals. But there was a deeper historical learning as well. The Russian economic historian Alexander Gerschenkron had argued in his theory of economic backwardness that countries that had not yet industrialised did not have to wait for the right conditions to appear. Gerschenkron had studied the development experience of Europe in great detail. He said that institutional innovation was the way forward for those who were late into the game: Germany had used investment banks to push its initial industrialisation, while Russia had used the state (he was referring to imperial Russia before the communists took over).[25]

This blinkered approach to industrial development was compounded by Nehru's prejudice against profit, which is the lifeblood of any business, private or public. In a well-known incident, J.R.D. Tata once tried to draw Nehru's attention to the poor state of public sector finances and pointed out that these companies, in which the government had invested so much capital, should be earning profits. Nehru did not take kindly to this advice. "Never talk to me about profit, Jeh. It is a dirty word," he said and turned to look outside the window, a clear signal that he was not interested in carrying this conversation forward.[26]

Nehru Ignores Small and Medium Enterprises

The logic of the Wage Goods Model could be extended to items of daily use such as sewing machines, bicycles, pencils, electric bulbs, footwear, garments, pots and pans, etc. The manufacture of these goods by small businessmen in India's smaller towns and cities could conceivably have provided employment to millions of people. This would have generated demand for a variety of goods and services, generated revenues for the government and decentralised the development paradigm.

Nehruvian planners made a token gesture towards small industries by reserving some items for the handloom and handicrafts sector. This also won them the support of the small but influential group of Gandhians who still held sway in some sections of society. But as an economic policy intervention it was a fig leaf, as the *charkha* could not compete with the modern textile industry.

What the Indian economy needed was a paradigm shift in the newly unveiled development narrative. It needed thousands of small and medium enterprises to make low value goods that could be produced by semi-skilled workers using low technology machines and tools and labour-intensive methods to absorb the millions of people who were eagerly waiting to be employed.

In Japan, SMEs manufacturing similar products had grouped together in the same geographical areas to form clusters. Each produced a particular component for a larger assembly. For example, one or two producers would make wheel rims for bicycles; another set of producers would make handlebars; a third set would make the spokes for the wheel, and so on. They would supply their components to an assembler who would put the bicycle together and ship it to the retailer for sale to the end customer.

India already had industry clusters in the Asansol–Durgapur belt of West Bengal, Ludhiana in Punjab, Coimbatore in Tamil Nadu, and Ahmedabad in Gujarat. They had gained considerable fame and prosperity supplying cycle and sewing machine parts, engineering goods and textiles to larger units within their catchment areas. Economic logic and empirical evidence from Japan and Europe suggested that the next stage in the development chain would be the emergence of companies making machines that could make the components before the final stage, which would see the birth of indigenous companies that could make those machines. This is how industries have organically developed all over the world.

But the Nehruvian model put the cart before the horse. Instead of building up the country's industrial foundation from the bottom up, with heavy machinery and steel making as the final step in the process, he placed heavy industry at the front and centre of his development architecture. This model was bound to fail, and it did.

Absence of Export Focus Cost India Dear

After the Second World War, as Japanese industry climbed up the value chain, opportunities began to appear at the lower end of the market. Japan had still not mastered the art of quality control, and many Japanese products were known for poor quality. With global trade expanding year upon year, India was ideally poised to gain from international trade. India even had a short-lived advantage over Japan. In the early 1950s, India had a larger share of world trade in manufactured items than Japan, which was still coming to terms with the devastation wrought by the Second World War. But the Japanese industry, with the active support of the post-war government of that country, soon came to dominate world trade in low-technology, labour-intensive items such as bicycles, textiles, toys, garments, and the like.

A rising tide lifts all boats, but Nehruvian planners did not even have a plan in place to benefit from the expansion of global commerce. As the Japanese manufacturing sector steadily mastered the quality and the technology to move up the value chain, opportunities opened up again for Indian industry in the late 1950s and 1960s, but the Nehru administration again missed the bus and allowed countries like Hong Kong, Singapore, Taiwan and South Korea to capture the market being vacated by Japan.

Experts and analysts have not been able to find a convincing explanation for Nehru's export pessimism. He was well travelled, well read, well exposed to the world at large. His circle of friends and acquaintances included some of the brightest minds in Europe and the US, and he had the extraordinary privilege of being able to turn to the best economists and academics in India and the world for advice.

One explanation places his aversion to international commerce to his belief in socialism. Widely regarded as a Fabian Socialist, who eschewed the rough edges and the extremism of classical Marxism, Nehru had, in fact, been far more radical in his beliefs till the mid-1930s. He firmly believed that capitalism was the path to imperialism since the leading capitalist countries of the time had large and small colonies that were the source of raw materials as well as the market for their finished products. The logic of this flawed argument dictated that growing international trade was, therefore, a stepping stone towards developing imperialist tendencies. "We wanted neither to be victims of an imperialist power nor to develop such tendencies ourselves," he wrote in *The Discovery of India.*[27]

Some scholars have explained his deep suspicion of foreign trade as a reaction to India's own experience of being colonised by a foreign trading company. Others explain the absence of an export thrust in the Nehruvian development paradigm as being dictated by the falling terms of trade for Third World countries because of falling commodity prices following the end of the Korean War. In 1963, a young economist called Manmohan Singh would point out a fatal flaw in Nehru's economic policy—the absence of any export thrust. In a delicious coincidence, Singh would preside over the dismantling of much of the Nehruvian economic edifice as Finance Minister between 1991 and 1996.

The First Five Year Plan, though, did have a small reference to exports. It said India should explore the potential for exporting low value goods such as bicycles, batteries, sewing machines and pharmaceuticals by raising the small volumes that it then sold to countries of Southeast Asia. That was it! Nehru and his advisors completely ignored exports after that.

Opportunity Missed: India's Share in Global Trade in Manufacturing Was Greater than Japan's

It is not well known—and Indian economic histories have airbrushed the fact—that in the early 1950s, India's share of world trade in manufactured products was slightly higher than Japan's.[28] In the years before and immediately after the Second World War, Japan had a plethora of small and medium-sized firms that were financially unstable and produced goods of inferior quality. They mostly made low-end, labour-intensive goods like bicycles, men's shirts, women's blouses, cheap toys and household items of daily use.

Till a few years ago, it was common for Indians to dismiss Chinese products as cheap and shoddy. "*Yeh Chinese maal jaise hai,*" was a common jibe aimed at substandard products. In the 1940s and early 1950s, Japanese products suffered a similar reputation in India. After the war, they began exporting mechanical toys and low-end appliances to countries in Asia while still exporting shirts and blouses to the U.S. and Europe. A Rochester (U.S.) newspaper carried a report in 1954 that claimed that Japanese-made toys were highly dangerous as they would burst into flames and give off toxic gases when placed near something hot.[29]

But Japan soon mastered the art of quality manufacturing and began to climb the global value chain. By the end of the decade, Japanese cameras, binoculars and other products began to enjoy a globally competitive reputation.

The early years after the Second World War was a period of learning for manufacturers around the world. Given the shortages in every country (barring the U.S.), there was a large tolerance for low-quality, low-end goods. This was an opportune time for Indian manufacturers to enter the global trade in low value goods and use its low cost of production to carve a niche for Indian products in the world markets.

The reconstruction of Europe, Japan, and South East Asia created an unprecedented boom for a wide range of products in the decade following the Second World War. As Japanese companies moved up the value and technology chains, they vacated the lower end of the market. Indian businesses could have used this period of tolerance to occupy this place and then scale up the quality and value ladder.

This window remained open all the way up to the 1980s. During this time, the Asian Tigers (South Korea, Taiwan, Singapore and Hong Kong), some of their ASEAN neighbours, and then China joined the global trade bandwagon by first plucking the low-hanging fruits and then moving up the value chain.

India missed the bus completely.

By the time it belatedly shed its Nehruvian legacy in 1991, there were no low-hanging fruits left to pluck. Since then, India has been playing catch-up.

So, who is to blame for India's failure to make a mark in global manufacturing exports? Should not the people who physically stopped Indian businesses from joining the global value chains and tied them up in red tape be held responsible?

The Main Beneficiaries Were Speculators

Walter Crocker was posted in India as Australian High Commissioner during the Nehru years. He spent close to a decade in this country and published a book titled *Nehru: A Contemporary's Estimate* in 1966. A keen observer of contemporary India, he said:

> Over two periods between 1952 and 1962, it was my job to watch Nehru day by day. Had my job in Delhi been anything else, I would have still watched him, out of interest, almost helpless interest. He was interesting because of his political importance but still more interesting because of himself.[30]

Like most neutral observers, Crocker had his reservations about Nehru's fascination with Five Year Plans. He wrote:

> As for what the plans will achieve, they will no doubt achieve—they are already achieving—some industrialisation and some increase in irrigation. This fact remains though, some of the industrialisation will be expensive for what it returns, and inefficient as well as jerry-built. Industry in India is high cost; reports have recently been published showing average factory costs at 40 per cent above British and still more above American costs. What the plans will assuredly achieve is to bring about still bigger cities and with bigger slums; Calcutta, for instance, conceivably growing from 6 million to 15 million. Planners never seem to think about planning cities.[31]

He also minced no words about the trajectory of India's economic development and whom it was benefitting. Far from benefitting the common man, the Nehruvian economic policies had exactly the opposite effect. Over the ten years that Crocker spent in India, inflation severely impacted people's purchasing power as prices almost doubled and taxation levels went up. "The classes which have benefited most have been the speculators (and) urban developers," observed Crocker.[32]

3

Raj-Era Bureaucracy Left Unreformed

Three years before he passed away in 1964, Jawaharlal Nehru was asked to identify his greatest failure as Prime Minister. He identified his failure to reform the bureaucracy as the biggest source of red ink on his administrative report card. "I failed to change the administration; it is still a colonial administration," he admitted.[33]

There is little evidence, though, that he made any serious effort at reforming the bureaucracy during his long, 17-year tenure as Prime Minister. In fact, it was his fascination with the Soviet model of development and planning, his policy of encouraging heavy industries, and the consequent rise of the license-permit raj that conferred unprecedented levels of discretionary powers on civil servants at every level of government.

This power was exercised by not only the elite Indian Administrative Service (IAS), the Indian Police Service (IPS) and other All India Services and Central Services but also by members of a vastly expanded bureaucracy that included hundreds of thousands of personnel with limited education and exposure who worked under lax supervision and weak systems of accountability. Commenting on the Indian bureaucracy soon after independence, the World Bank wrote:

"The competence of higher civil servants stands comparison with that of any country in the world," but "there is far too much lethargy, indifference and a lack of urgency among the lower ranks of officials who come into daily contact with the public."[34]

That is a rather severe indictment of a service that had succeeded the Imperial Civil Service (ICS) that British Prime Minister David Lloyd George had called the "steel frame" in a House of Commons debate in 1921. This description soon gained currency and popular resilience and came to define the self-image as well as the public perception of the service.

Ironically, it was Nehru who seemed least enamoured of this steel frame. Prior to becoming Prime Minister and the de facto master of the civil services, he had made no bones about the fact that he wanted British India's civil services dismantled.

In his autobiography published in 1936, he wrote:

> But of one thing I am quite sure, that no new order can be built up in India as long as the spirit of the ICS pervades our administration and our public services... Therefore, it seems to me quite essential that the ICS and similar services must disappear completely, as such, before we can start real work on a new order.[35]

A letter to Sardar Patel a decade later, when he was Vice President of the Viceroy's Executive Council, showed that he had not changed his mind in the intervening years:

> ...our troubles may be due to lack of system or policy, apart from individuals... decisions taken are not given effect to and are hung up inordinately. It is difficult to catch the culprits for some suitable excuse is always

> forthcoming. I am shocked at the slowness of our work and the delays that continually occur. I felt, therefore, and still feel that it is necessary to overhaul this entire system.[36]

But despite such lofty declarations of intent, Nehru did precious little to reform the bureaucracy that independent India had inherited from the British Raj. Yes, the name of ICS was changed to IAS and IP became IPS. But that apart, he made no serious effort to change the basic structure and orientation of the services. The procedures, rules, precedents and practices of the British era continued to inform the civil services of independent India.

The Fundamental Rules and Supplementary Rules were first compiled in 1922 and continue to govern the service of government servants.[37] The Indian Police Act 1861, which was even older, governed the constabulary across the country. A colonial civil service, set up by a colonial government to rule over—as opposed to serve—the Indian people continued to hold sway unreformed over the citizens of the newly independent nation. Thus, the outlook and orientation of the civil servants who administered the country continued to remain steeped in the colonial mentality.

The lynchpin of the colonial administration outside of the big cities was the District Magistrate or Collector. This officer was tasked with several responsibilities, but his two main jobs were collection of revenues and the maintenance of law and order. These young ICS officers were quite clearly the ruling class, and the architecture of the service and the social milieu of the Raj ensured that they remained a cut above the rest. More than seventy years later, very little has changed.

If one were to look even cursorily at the leading civil servants who held important positions in the Nehru administration one will find an overwhelming number who came from the upper classes of Indian society. A majority of them had been to similar schools and colleges (some admittedly on scholarships) and a significant number of them were influenced by the spirit of the times which was suspicious of business and entrepreneurs.

These bureaucrats retained the governance template of the British Raj and with the Prime Minister's blessings put in place systems that willy-nilly discouraged efficiency, competition, and employment generation. Not surprisingly, these policies did not succeed in achieving the desired levels of growth; they also failed spectacularly to achieve the government's social goals, enabled the creation of private and public sector monopolies and saddled the Indian economy with hundreds of inefficient plants with sub-optimal capacities. Worse, entrepreneurs no longer had the final word on the location of the factories or the technology that would go into it. In many cases, these decisions were also taken by civil servants sitting in government offices who had very little clue about the issues involved.

What Lee Kew Yuan Did Differently

Nehru's inability or unwillingness to initiate bureaucratic reforms and get into the minutiae of governance contrasts starkly with the example of Singapore's legendary leader Lee Kew Yuan. In his memoirs, he wrote:

> "My experience of developments in Asia has led me to conclude that we need good men to have good government.

> However good the system of government, bad leaders will bring harm to their people... The single decisive factor that made for Singapore's development was the ability of its ministers and the high quality of the civil servants who supported them."[38]

In his endeavour to improve systems and governance in Singapore, Lee did not hesitate to draw best practices from diverse sources such as the civil services of Japan and France and petroleum giant Shell's performance appraisal system. He consulted the leaders of several multinational companies on their recruitment and promotion policies and admitted to adopting the Shell Company's system for his government's bureaucracy in 1983 "after trying out the Shell system and finding it practical and reliable," as he said in his memoirs.[39]

Unlike Nehru, who resorted to rhetoric and appeals to idealism to exhort people to engage in the task of nation building, Lee adopted a policy of offering them material incentives. "If we underpay men of quality as ministers, we cannot expect them to stay long in office earning a fraction of what they could outside... Underpaid ministers and public officials have ruined many governments in Asia," he observed in his memoirs. This practical, down-to-earth wisdom is starkly absent in Nehru's thinking.

Singapore, like India, was a poor country when it gained independence in 1959 and, therefore, could not afford to pay its civil servants very high salaries. However, when the government's free market policies began to show results in the 1970s, it began to raise their compensation in order to continue to attract the best and the brightest talent. The higher salaries coupled with stringent anti-corruption laws also incentivised these public administrators not to eschew the straight and narrow path. When a 1981 survey by Singapore's Internal Revenue Department showed private sector salaries to be significantly higher than what the government was offering, Lee's administration responded by raising the salaries of its bureaucrats in 1982, 1988, 1989 and 1994 to bridge the gap.[40]

Explaining Lee's rationale, his son Lee Hsien Loong, then Singapore's Minister for Trade and Industry, said on March 17, 1989, that the government believed in paying "civil servants market rates for their abilities and responsibilities" and that it "will offer whatever salaries are necessary to attract and retain the talent that it needs… Paying civil servants adequate salaries is absolutely essential to maintain the quality of public administration."[41]

Contrast this with the ideologically blinkered approach of the Indian government. Lee was, thus, using the profit motive as a carrot to incentivise bureaucrats to perform to the best of their abilities. This practical and visionary stand contrasts with Nehru's ideological and self-defeating suspicion of personal gain and his dubbing profit a "dirty word."

Edgar Henry Schein, Professor at the MIT Sloan School of Management and foundational researcher in the discipline of organisational behaviour, has credited Singapore's success to its highly competent and motivated civil service, which attracts "the best and brightest" citizens into its ranks. The consistently high scores of the Singapore bureaucracy in the World Bank's governance indicators is a reflection of this reality.

Every leader faces the challenges of location, resources, legacy issues and international relations. How they stand up to these and manage their responsibilities determines their legacies. Lee transformed a tiny city state with no natural resources and questionable potential into a first world country in a short span of four decades. That, any neutral observer will accept, is a sign of a great visionary leader. India, unfortunately, lacked such leaders with vision, ambition and ability in the first four decades of its independence.

Status Quo Continues After Independence

The top leadership of newly independent India did not display the nimble footedness and vision that Lee did in Singapore more than a decade later, and this ensured that the Indian bureaucracy became an instrument for the perpetuation of the status quo.

Sadly, the atrophy that had begun to set in during the Nehru years has continued till present times. N.C. Saxena, who retired as Secretary, Planning Commission of India in 2002, and also served in the mid-1990s as Director, National Academy of Administration, Mussoorie, which trains civil servants, writes in his book *What Ails the IAS and Why It Fails to Deliver*:

> A high degree of professionalism ought to be the dominant characteristic of a modern bureaucracy. The fatal failing of the Indian bureaucracy has been its low level of professional competence. The IAS officer spends more than half of his tenure on policy desks where domain knowledge is a vital prerequisite. However, in the present environment, there is no incentive for a young civil servant to acquire knowledge or to improve their skills. As years pass by,

> there is thus an exponential growth in both his ignorance and arrogance.[42]

Interestingly, noted economist I.G. Patel, who was a member of the Indian Economic Service and who served as Special Secretary in the Ministry of Finance and Secretary, Economic Affairs, Ministry of Finance, Government of India—and, most importantly, as the Governor of the Reserve Bank of India—said that Nehru's

> acceptance of controls came through the influence of civil servants, who had gone to the same kind of schools and who spoke the same kind of English and with whom, as a result, he came to have a special kind of rapport.[43]

The likes of Sir N.R. Pillai, Y.N. Sukthankar, Vishnu Sahay (who had two separate terms as Cabinet Secretary) and M.K. Vellodi served as the country's leading civil servants under Nehru. All these distinguished men came from similar class backgrounds, had studied at the most elite institutions; some of them had pursued higher studies in England and at least one of them hailed from royalty.

Nehru's comfort with the bureaucracy after independence and his reluctance to reform it can be traced back to his own upbringing, which was very Anglicised and Westernised. His father Motilal Nehru had been an ardent admirer of the British, and the seven years he spent in England as a student left a deep, lifelong impression on Nehru. "I imbibed most of the prejudices of Harrow and Cambridge. And in my likes and dislikes, I was perhaps more an Englishman than an Indian," he wrote.[44]

It was not just a passing influence in youth. He admitted quite frankly that Western thinking had seeped into him and influenced the core of his being. He wrote in *The Discovery of India*:

> I approached her [India] almost as an alien critic, full of dislike for the present as well as for many of the relics of the past that I saw. To some extent, I came to her via the West, and looked at her as a friendly Westerner might have done.[45]

Given this cultural alienation that was his lifelong companion, it was not surprising that he found comfort in a cohort of civil servants who came from the same milieu and shared his cultural and social prejudices. In an article in *The Wire* titled "How Bureaucracy Has Left the Indian Civil Services Adrift," Amit Cowshish, former Financial Advisor (Acquisitions), Ministry of Defence, wrote: "Most officers assume the trappings of feudal grandeur much like their colonial predecessors, but without either their efficiency, commitment, or impartiality."[46]

Sycophancy, Intrigue, Corruption and Worse…

Writing the Nehru blog in *India Today*, dated June 15, 1984, Suman Dubey noted:

> One single statistical detail reveals the grim fall-out. According to a Home Ministry study, in the 1950s, the average tenure of an IAS officer in a posting was 48 months. This came down to 38 months in the '60s and 21 months in the '70s. The main reason: punitive transfers.
>
> Small wonder that there is a rising eagerness in the civil services to seek premature retirement. As the Indian

> Express commented editorially last fortnight: "The civil services have been politicised and independent and honest administrators often find it difficult to survive in an atmosphere of sycophancy, intrigue, corruption and worse.... It is the careerist who flourishes or others who are prepared to shut their eyes and drift. The rot has gone deep and must be arrested. The responsibility rests on the political leadership."
>
> Some of the responsibility rests with Nehru's generation too, for not seeing the need to reform the administrative system. Experiments with community development and panchayati raj were abandoned once it became clear that they wouldn't easily mesh with the civil administration inherited from the colonial era, and the systems of government and politics already in existence.[47]

This is not the opinion of a Nehru family baiter. It comes from an insider of the charmed inner circle that surrounds it.

British Era Mindset Remained Unreformed

This mindset, which pervaded the ICS and other arms of the Raj-era bureaucracy, remained largely unreformed as the political leadership made no effort to bring about a cultural change in the civil service. Little wonder, then, that large sections of ordinary Indians continued to feel alienated from the administration. Most accounts of the civil services from the immediate post-independence era talk of bureaucrats as "brown sahibs" who had little in common socially, culturally or emotionally with the people they were mandated to serve.

Leaving the civil services unreformed allowed the class bias inherent within it to play out with each passing year—

and this had a deleterious effect on India's development journey. Michael Lipton's 1977 book, *Why Poor People Stay Poor: A Study of Urban Bias in World Development*, sheds light on this phenomenon. The author provocatively declared that "the most important class conflict is not between labour and capital. Nor is it between foreign and national interests. It is between the rural classes and the urban classes."[48] He showed how economic growth across the world, since the Second World War, had disproportionately benefitted urban communities and how rural poverty had increased. He also demonstrated that both neo-classical as well as Marxist economics suffer from this urban bias. Specifically singling out India, Lipton argued that investments and foreign aid had gone overwhelmingly to towns and cities, which was inequitable and unjust to rural areas. The bias against rural areas also showed up in price, tax and educational policies as well as research expenditures. This urban bias was a result of the power of the urban elite and their rural allies as well as a mindset that displayed disdain for the peasantry. Given the class composition of the senior bureaucracy under Nehru, it was not surprising that no one complained about the lack of effort to reform the civil services.

Walter Crocker also estimated that it was the Prime Minister's urban mindset and the resulting disconnect with rural India that could be the cause of the government's failure to set up an efficient model of governance of which bureaucratic reforms is a very important component.

> The Five-Year Plans reflect the urban mind. Nehru, like most Indian politicians, was urban. Outside of their towns the politicians are like fish without water. This is why

> agriculture, though given thousands of pages, millions of words, and various huge schemes, such as community development or the Grow More Food campaigns, was not given enough effective action... As for the Nehru plans considered specifically, and apart from the general strategy, they run into hundreds of different projects ranging from small technical schools to big hydroelectric schemes but they have tended to be too imprecise in their priorities or aims; too lacking in a groundwork of intellectual and then solid technical preparation... too much defectiveness in execution so that there has been a shortfall as regards many, perhaps, most targets, and virtual failures.[49]

Three decades later, little had changed. In her book titled *Durbar*, journalist, columnist and author Tavleen Singh wrote how, in the late 1970s, the senior ranks of the Indian bureaucracy were still filled with mostly upper middle class individuals, many of whom took great pride in their Oxbridge accents and Westernised ways. Several of them were more at home with English than their native tongues and had disdain for their ministers and their often rustic ways. Not surprisingly, she writes, this snobbish lot carried tales of how their ministers would slurp their tea from saucers and pick their noses in the presence of others.[50] Given this class bias, it is not hard to imagine their opinions of the common people they were mandated to service. It was little wonder then that India had failed to achieve any of the lofty social and economic goals it had targeted since Independence. Despite democracy and universal adult franchise, the difference between the rulers and the ruled was clear and stark—and Nehru and his successors did nothing to change this.

Committed Bureaucracy and Their Disdain for the Common Man

Indira Gandhi's push for a "committed bureaucracy," which was nothing but shorthand for civil servants who were committed to perpetuating her rule, had considerably whittled away the independence of India's so-called "iron frame."

Tavleen Singh, who has been an insider in Delhi's power circle for decades and has had the opportunity to observe several leading politicians and bureaucrats and their families from close quarters, wrote about how she believes the Indian bureaucracy has supported the Nehru–Gandhi family: "High officials in India are famous for the disdain with which they treat the representatives of the people but put them in the presence of a member of the Gandhi family and they behave like humble employees."[51]

But, she added, the Gandhis have been very selective about admitting civil servants into their inner circle.

> ...but on the edge of their courts have always lurked senior bureaucrats dripping with servility they rarely show anyone else. The most sycophantic are those that went to Oxford and Cambridge and who appear to have developed from this British experience a genetic memory of serving colonial masters.[52]

This was a trait in Indian civil servants that was already becoming evident in the 1950s. Given Nehru's messianic zeal to secure the commanding heights of the Indian economy for the public sector and his mistrust of the private sector, it did not take long for Congress politicians and civil servants alike to realise that an easy way to get into the Prime Minister's good books was to design and implement policies to stifle private enterprise in pursuit of the ephemeral "socialistic pattern of society."

By this time, Nehru had lost his earlier enthusiasm for bureaucratic reforms. He told a journalist in 1959: "I think the services, by and large, are very good... what is really wrong is not the human material but the procedures inherited by us from the past."[53]

He was also aware that the bureaucracy was the not geared towards efficient delivery of services and was more interested in safeguarding its self-interest. He was also conscious that the services were growing in size without any commensurate improvement in the quality of delivery. He observed:

> The way government organizations and departments multiply leads us nowhere but to waste... If it is not stopped, I tell you, the head will remain small while the body will go in increasing in size. Such maldevelopment of organizations is dangerous to our country.[54]

His inability or unwillingness to reform the bureaucracy has extracted a very heavy price. The rot that had begun to set in then has now become institutionalised. This is proving to be a drag on India's development plans. In their book *Corruption in India: The DNA and RNA*, Bibek Debroy and Laveesh Bhandari estimated that India is losing as much $12 billion per year through bureaucratic corruption.

India's global image is also taking a beating on this count. "We estimate that if India were to pursue civil service reforms and reach the Asian average on government effectiveness, it could add 0.9 percentage points annually to per capita GDP... Institutional quality is a crucial driver of economic performance," a 2014 Goldman Sachs report said.[55]

In a serious indictment of the ways of the Indian bureaucracy, Milan Vaishanav and Saksham Khosla of Carnegie Endowment said in their study on the IAS:

> Globally, there is a robust, positive relationship between the quality of government and economic progress. But India has experienced rapid growth in spite of below-par governance. Indeed, the quality of India's public-sector institutions in particular has struggled to keep pace with the country's rapid economic advancement. As the adage goes, "India grows at night while the government sleeps."[56]

These indictments largely refer to recent developments but the observations are equally applicable to the period under review.

Why Nehru Failed to Reform the Bureaucracy

Some analysts and historians have attempted to analyse why Nehru failed to reform the bureaucracy despite his fervent belief that such a course of action was a necessary prerequisite for building the egalitarian and developed India of his dreams. They point to the fact that the partition had left the civil services in a very precarious position. About half of the 1,200 ICS officers were British, and they departed with the colonial masters. Another 100 or so officers opted for Pakistan, leaving only about 500 civil servants, i.e. less than half the required number of senior civil servants to govern 300 million people and address the series of crises that arose: the refugee problem, the communal conflagration, and the resulting law and order and humanitarian challenges.

We get a glimpse into his thinking on the matter from a letter he wrote to his sister Krishna Hutheesing on November 1, 1947, i.e. just over two months after independence:

> It is difficult for me to explain to you the situation here, and the difficulties we have to face all around. It has been impossible in these circumstances to do many of the things we wanted to do. All planning has been postponed. We live here from crisis to crisis and all planning has been postponed.[57]

By the late 1950s, a decade of being at the helm of affairs had taken its toll on his enthusiasm for bringing about a change in the governance paradigm. His administration displayed a marked lack of innovation in dealing with a bureaucracy that was designed to ensure stability rather than bring about change. The Weberian concept of bureaucracy—on which the Indian Civil Service was based—was focused on stability, efficiency and continuity. S.S. Gill, a career bureaucrat and a Padma Bhushan, who retired as Secretary, Ministry of Information and Broadcasting in 1985, noted:

> But after Independence, the basic theme of the country's polity were change, transformation and reform... By retaining the colonial bureaucracy, Nehru inadvertently adopted a system which placed a heavy premium on status quo... In its working, bureaucracy manifests the power of the state. But pursuit of power becomes an end itself. Though it continuously interacts with the people and deals with their problems, its elitist character inhibits the fostering of warmth and empathy towards them. Cultivation of an impersonal and detached approach turns the administrative act into a clinical exercise instead of a

> human encounter. It keeps proliferating not in response to demand, but as a means to self-aggrandizement.[58]

The progressive Prime Minister with fire in his belly and radical reform in his heart had metamorphosed into a status quoist leader who now found solace in socialist rhetoric and an elite coterie of advisors that had had a vested interest in perpetuating the status quo that guaranteed their positions at the top of the pyramid even as the teeming masses below them continued to suffer. Reforming the administrative architecture to strengthen and streamline the delivery of services was too difficult a task to accomplish and so, was given a quiet burial.

Nehru's lament that he had failed to reform the bureaucracy must be countered with a question: did he even make any effort to bring about the changes required to alter the mindset of the civil service and transform it from an instrument of foreign rule to a platform designed the serve the people of India? The sad answer is: no! Despite the soaring rhetoric and the flowery language, Nehru had unfortunately become a front for and a standard bearer of the very status quo that he had set out to overturn. It is one of history's ironies that Nehru's rule came to resemble what Gandhi had warned against: English rule without the Englishmen.

4

Neglect of Education Condemned Generations of Indians to Poverty

NEW DELHI: Nobel laureate Amartya Sen on Monday regretted a lackadaisical approach to primary education since Independence and pitched for enhanced government focus on the sector for robust economic growth.

Praising Jawaharlal Nehru for his pioneering role for the growth of technical education in the country, Sen said the late Prime Minister's attitude for primary education was, however, "lamentable".

"Although Nehru had the understanding of primary education, and was committed to it, in terms of channelling resources, priorities or planning, there was a big failure," said Amartya Sen. "His attitude to primary education was deeply lamentable in my view, but he did understand one thing, the importance of technical education," he said.

He added that though India has many achievements in the success of a small group of privileged people who are well trained in higher education and specialised expertise, "yet our educational system remains deeply unjust".

PTI. July 4, 2011

When it came to choosing a secondary board for my daughter, my wife and I were in a dilemma. After consulting friends and well-wishers, we selected the IGCSE stream for her. Years later, we are really happy that we made the right choice.

Unlike most Indian boards, the process of teaching under this board gave her an independent mind but did not impose any particular line of thought on her. She had to research issues from sources outside her prescribed books, learn thesis writing, and the art of making presentations. In subjects like history and global perspectives, she had to analyse historical and contemporary events. There were no right or wrong answers. She had to take a stand one way or the other and justify it both logically and from a historical perspective. (This would have created a furore in some other schools; parents would have screamed "out of syllabus.") This teaching method was an eye-opener for me. It taught my daughter how to think rather than what to think and did not lay much stress on memorising texts. And that, I think, is the crucial difference between how we were taught and how these foreign boards teach.

And that perhaps is the reason why Indians make great software developers but not great innovators. Our education system is designed to kill all curiosity and the spirit of enquiry from an early age. The system privileges memorisation and rote learning, and sticks to a syllabus that proactively discourages questions and punishes independent thinking. Deviations from this norm are penalised. Scoring high marks is the only goal that students are taught to aim for. Gaining knowledge becomes a secondary and often irrelevant endeavour for most.

By the time they finish their studies, most students learn to value conformity, having been forced to bury their spirit of curiosity and innovation on the way up the education ladder from Class 1 onwards. The system effectively squeezes out all original thought and mass produces graduates, many of whom are unprepared to face a world where questions do not come out of a set syllabus.

This is a critical failure of our education system—the inability to produce a large enough cohort of students who can indulge in lateral thinking and chart out trails on which others have not walked before. The students should not be held responsible for this. It is the syllabus designers who have a lot to answer for.

Can you name a single scientist, economist, or intellectual who is a genuinely famous across the world for work done in India in the post-Independence period? Can you name a single scientific breakthrough that has come out of India after Independence?

The only world-famous scientists who have made globally-recognised breakthroughs lived and worked in pre-Independence India—Acharya Jagadish Chandra Bose, C.V. Raman, Satyen Bose, and Meghnad Saha come to mind immediately. Others who achieved great global renown—Hargovind Khurana, Amartya Sen, Abhijit Banerjee, Subrahmanyan Chandrasekhar, and a handful of others—spent their entire professional lives abroad and carried out their research in foreign universities. So, a large part of the credit for their achievements must go to the enabling environment that encouraged innovation and independent thinking.

Far from encouraging innovation, the "system" in India proactively blocks breakthroughs and hounds independent thinkers. My father's friend and colleague, Dr Subhash Mukherjee, created the world's second test-tube baby in Calcutta in 1978, just 67 days after the birth of Louise, the world's first such baby in England.[59]

The West Bengal government was hostile to him from the outset. It set up a committee to validate Dr Mukherjee's claims. The members of the committee had no expertise in IVF.[60] Meanwhile, the Union government refused him the permission to attend international conferences.

The movie *Ek Doctor Ki Maut* directed by Tapan Sinha records his travails. Far from feting Dr Mukherjee and giving him a Padma award, he was called a fraud, his work was labelled "unbelievable," and "bogus," and he was hounded and insulted. Unable to take the humiliation, he died by suicide on June 19, 1981.[61] I remember my father being very upset. He commented wryly: "Subhash shouldn't have come back to India. In England, he would probably have been knighted and invited to have dinner with the Queen."

Recognition and rehabilitation came too late for him when in 1997, i.e. sixteen years after his passing, T.C. Anand Kumar, Director of IRR (ICMR), credited with creating India's second test-tube baby, was given access to Dr Mukherjee's papers on a visit to Kolkata. It was only after he validated Dr Mukherjee's experiment that the truth emerged.[62]

Dr Dhaniram Barua, who performed the world's first pig heart transplant on a human being in January 1997 was hounded and jailed. His patient lived for seven days after the transplant, proving that pig-to-human organ transplants were possible. Instead of encouraging further research for what was truly a global first, the government hounded him, charged him with homicide[63], and arrested him for 40 days before he was granted bail.[64] Twenty-five years later, on January 7, 2022, doctors at the University of Maryland Medical School in the US performed what is considered the world's first successful transplant of a genetically modified pig heart in a 57-year-old man.[65] Mind you, the recipient in the US transplant, David Bennet, passed away 8 March 2022[66], less than two months after his transplant. No doctor was arrested, no one was hounded

These cases sent a chilling message to all innovators and independent thinkers: Don't you dare do anything original and cutting edge. You will be punished. If this is how India treats innovators, it will have to remain satisfied with imported technology. Innovators will go abroad with their billion-dollar ideas and the authorities and the media will continue to rue the copy-and-paste models of Indian tech entrepreneurs.

This is why genuine scientific breakthroughs have not taken place in India post-independence. This points to a greater and more fundamental failure—of our education system in creating an environment that encourages enquiry. Fortunately, though, the situation is changing for the better under the current Indian government.

The Historical Context

It is now widely accepted that British rule was disastrous for India. Not only did the colonial masters drain India of its resources, they also made very little effort to equip Indians to face the future. Far from being the enlightened and benevolent rulers they claimed to be, the colonial masters left India as an emaciated and impoverished shadow of the wealthy, if fractious and divided, country they came to rule over gradually from 1757. If British rule were indeed enlightened as our colonial masters claimed, why was India poor, largely illiterate, and mostly hungry in 1947?

Nowhere is the deleterious effect of colonial rule more evident than in the field of education. The British system of education was designed to produce a class of intermediaries who would help the colonial masters perpetuate their rule in this country. It was not intended to educate people to question the status quo or encourage independent thinking. Not surprisingly, the system produced a thin layer of well-educated Indians. Below this paper-thin elite sliver of society was a marginally larger slice of society that received rudimentary education, which enabled them to get lower-level jobs in the government and the private sector. The rest of India—comprising more than eight out of ten Indians—was left without any education or hope.

In the mid-eighteenth century, when Britain began to conquer and rule parts of India, the literacy rate in Britain was about 60 percent. By the middle of the twentieth century, that figure had maxed out at 100 percent. In India, we do not have any reliable figures for literacy in 1757, but, in 1947, when the British left, only about 16 percent of the population was literate. As noted above, a tiny sliver of India's upper classes was highly educated. But below this level, there was a widespread lack of formal education. That is hardly a healthy report card for the so-called enlightened European rule.

Education: The Panacea for India's Backwardness

Independence presented an opportunity to make a clean break from the dismal record of the colonial masters. The new leadership of independent India was educated, liberal, and committed to lifting the lot of the Indian people. The Koreans had, by the 1950s, marched far ahead of India; more than 50 percent of their respective populations were literate and they were investing aggressively in spreading education throughout all sections of the population, especially among the female population.

Nehru had noted with dismay in his magnum opus *The Discovery of India* how millions of Indian aspirations were stunted or remained stillborn because of a lack of education. He wrote:

> Of our millions how few get any education at all, how many live on the verge of starvation; of even those who get some education how many have nothing to look forward to but a clerkship in some office on a pay that is usually far less than the unemployment dole in England. If life opened its gates to them and offered them food and healthy conditions of living and education and opportunities of growth, how many among these millions would be eminent scientists, educationists, technicians, industrialists, writers and artists, helping to build a new India and a new world?[67]

Rhetoric Was Divorced from Reality

It was fair to expect the leadership of independent India to focus on educating the masses and, thus, energise the Indian population to pursue a higher purpose. History, it seemed, had placed the right man, Nehru, in the right place—in the

Prime Minister's office—to deliver the Indian people from their ignorance. After a thousand years of conquest and servitude, a happy confluence of circumstances seemed to signal a happy augury for the Indian people as he seemed to have been chosen by destiny to open life's gates for them.

His rhetoric, full of empathy and concern, was politically correct. "Our effort must be to bring about equality among the people by providing equal opportunity for education and employment," he said in 1954.[68] This was a basic precondition for egalitarian development, a fact that had been acknowledged even by Adam Smith, who is known as the father of modern economics for his theories on demand and supply, capitalism and free markets. People even in "the lowest of occupations must acquire the essential parts of education—to read, write, and account—before they can be employed...," he wrote.

Two centuries later, in *A Memorandum to the Government of India 1955*, noted economist Milton Friedman, who had been engaged as a consultant by the Ministry of Finance, said:

> The great untapped resource of technical and scientific knowledge available to India for the taking is the economic equivalent of the untapped continent available to the United States 150 years ago. The basic question is one of method. The belief that underlies these notes is that the basic requisites are... greatly widened opportunities for education and training... and an environment that gives maximum scope to the initiative and energy of farmers, businessmen, and traders.[69]

So, Nehru had intellectual validation from one of the world's foremost economists who had been engaged by his government. Yet, he chose to ignore the advice of experts.

An insight into his priorities can be inferred from the allocation of funds in the first, second, and third Five Year Plans. The education budget in these—Nehru's signature blueprint for the development of India—ranged between 5.9 percent and 7.8 percent. Building the long-term potential of the Indian people was clearly not as important to him as other sectors such as industry, agriculture and communication, which promised, but did not deliver, immediate returns. These sectors got as much as double or triple the funds allocated to education. To make matters worse, when profligacy, poor planning, shoddy execution and corruption led to regular shortage of funds, it was invariably education that found its allocation reduced by as much as half over a period of time.

Nehru, Indira Squarely to Blame

Soon, this became the norm. India has traditionally spent about 3 percent of GNP on education. Little wonder that it has a third of the world's illiterates—the highest population of illiterate people in the world.[70] The blame for this shameful situation must lie squarely with Nehru and his daughter Indira Gandhi and their lopsided priorities. By neglecting education, they ensured that the foundations of India's development story would remain shaky for decades to come and even the best efforts of successor governments to close the gap with other countries would remain hamstrung by this academic drag. It is a matter of great embarrassment that countries like Sri Lanka, Egypt, Kenya as well as Southeast Asian nations like Indonesia, Malaysia and Thailand, among others, have much higher literacy rates than India.[71]

Nehru and Indira must also take the blame for the government's neglect of primary education. The First Five Year Plan had allocated 58 percent of the education budget to primary education, signalling that the planners knew where the problem lay. This provision dropped sharply by 40 percent for the Second Plan and again slipped further for the Third Plan.[72] The allocation for higher education (higher secondary, university level and technical education) grew from 35 percent in the First Plan to 60 percent and higher in the next two.

The rot in education began to set in with the Second Five Year Plan. The focus of the government shifted clearly and decisively in favour of heavy industries. Education was among the losers of the government's changed priorities. Its share of Plan funding fell from 7.9 percent to 5.9 percent, indicating in no uncertain terms that Nehruvian planners had decided to downgrade the importance of education. Within this reduced allocation, primary education was the biggest casualty—its share of funding within the education budget fell from 56 percent to 35 percent, as mentioned earlier. This was particularly surprising given that the Plan document accepted the poor learning outcomes of existing methods of pedagogy—more than half the students who joined the first grade did not complete the fourth grade and poor teacher quality continued to hobble the system.

How can one explain a firm believer in egalitarianism like Nehru signing off on this? The only plausible explanations for this apparent paradox are his elite upbringing, his fascination with science, his intellectual grounding in Harrow and Cambridge and the thought process these engendered. It also reflects the priorities of his elite band of bureaucrats who were his primary advisors as well as the executors of his plans. It does leave Nehru open to the charge of deliberately weakening the intellectual foundation of the Indian people and, thus, irretrievably setting back India's overall development agenda.

Political scientist Myron Weiner attempted to explain this neglect of primary education by blaming Indian "beliefs" about the "social order." Though he did not say explicitly say so, some people have interpreted this to mean that India's caste system and that the stranglehold of the elite on decision making could be holding back the spread of education among children from the less fortunate sections of society..[73] But, like the term Hindu rate of growth, this was just another dishonest intellectual attempt to blame Hindu traditions for the Nehru government's failures and shield the real culprits behind India's poor education outcomes.

Prolonged neglect of primary education was impacting outcomes quite negatively. This was acknowledged by the Education Ministry publication from 1985 titled *Challenge of Education*: "Many studies have shown that in the field of education, investments in elementary education yield the highest rate of returns and have a significant impact on productivity and general well being of the masses."[74]

Where Are the Educated Women?

Indian planners did not pay heed to American economist and diplomat John Kenneth Galbraith's profound words: "There is no literate population that is not developed, no illiterate population that is other than developed."[75]

Education is universally recognised as the real differentiator—in a world beset with stark inequalities, a good education can bring about a positive turnaround in the fortunes of an individual, a society, or an entire nation. Good education results in the creation of a more responsive and aware citizenry, the results of which can be seen across various facets of life. It is widely acknowledged as the most potent force to fight poverty, inequality and discrimination. Therefore, denial of "good" education opportunities not only amounts to injustice to generations of Indians but also goes against democratic principles of offering everyone an equal opportunity to progress.

The Asian nations to the east of India, on the other hand, focused sharply on educating their populations, and especially on women's enrolment. Good quality primary education to both male and female students produced industrial workers and farmers who were more adept at absorbing the latest technologies and practices and this resulted in these countries being able to produce increasingly better-quality goods for the world markets. The universalisation of education also helped them reduce inequality and poverty.[76] One more positive spin-off from this improvement in education levels was the rise in the percentage of women who joined the workforce. The truism that when you educate a woman you educate the entire family and the next generation as well held good as these women gave birth to fewer children and also invested more time, attention and effort on educating their children, thus, continuing the virtuous cycle of prosperity.

The examples of other Asian countries are illustrative of the positive spinoffs that women's education brings to societies. All the countries of East and Southeast Asia first achieved universal primary education for women before they could take off economically. Japan reached this target in the 1930s; tiger economies Taiwan and South Korea achieved universal primary education for women in the 1950s and 1960s, respectively. And the world has seen how China, which was in the same boat as India, zoomed ahead of every other Asian country after it managed to educate its female population.

There is enough and more empirical evidence to prove that women's education is *sine qua non* for an industrially educated workforce. That's because an educated woman results not only in an educated family but also in multi-generational transmission of education, which ensures a steady supply of educated workers over the long term.[77]

In fact, the East Asian success in the export market owes a lot to its well-educated female workforce. Women's participation in the labour force in the electronics, garments, footwear and textiles sectors in these countries is exceptionally high. This sequence—of universal primary education for women, followed by the development of export-focused labour-oriented industries—has been witnessed in several countries across Asia. In fact, the sequence of women's education, their entry into the workforce and the economic uplift of society as a whole dates to the years after the Industrial Revolution.

Arno Pearse, General Secretary of the International Federation of Textile Producers Association said of the Japanese mills in the late 1920s: "One notices everywhere the results of a good general education. Every mill girl reads, writes, and possesses a general education on par with that of most European countries." This, he said, led to less defective work and easier adoption of new technologies that further enhanced productivity and output.[78]

Michael Kremer, Professor of Economics at MIT, published a research paper in 1993, wherein he explained the wide range of productivity in different countries was due to variations in their levels of education. His paper proposed that more educated workers were more likely to be able to absorb new skills and make fewer errors. When they worked with others, such workers also improved each other's efficiency and effectiveness. This encouraged innovation and resulted in greater efficiency and a higher level of productivity.[79]

Nehru would have known of the Japanese example and would have been aware of the strides made by Taiwan on this count in the late 1950s. Indira Gandhi had these and the examples of other East and Southeast Asian countries to go by. Yet, their governments made no attempt to replicate this model in India. As a result of this unforgiveable administrative and policy failure on their part, India will now have to run twice as fast as the rest of its neighbours to play catch up with the world.

Education Was Not a Priority for Indira

Despite their socialist ideology and egalitarian rhetoric, both Nehru and his daughter Indira Gandhi failed to provide India's vast population equality of opportunity to educate itself and, thus, acquire the means to lift themselves out of the circumstances that destiny had placed them in. If Nehru's administration paid only lip service to the delivery of public goods such as health and education, Indira clearly indicated that these were not priorities that exercised her at all.

"I don't know how important literacy is. What has it done for the West? Are people happier or more alive to problems? On the contrary I think they've become more superficial," she told Mary Carras, an American academic who was writing a political biography on her.[80] This would seem to indicate cynicism and an innate unwillingness to genuinely empower the people. Could it be that she subscribed to the view that uneducated people were likely to be more docile and would, therefore, pose less of a threat to her continued political hegemony? Given her propensity to concentrate all power in herself, it is entirely possible that she felt insecure about an educated, enlightened electorate judging her performance on merit and voting accordingly. It would be in keeping with her personality and track record if she wanted to be in a position to give people a proverbial slice of fish and keep them beholden to her rather than teaching them how to fish, which would have given them the agency to act independently should they want to do so.

Mrs Gandhi recognised the failure of Nehru's education policy but chose not to take any measures to address its shortcomings. Given her lack of commitment to education, it was not, perhaps, surprising that she was not ready to invest the time, money, effort and political capital needed to overhaul the country's primary education system. It could have been done "when we became free," she said, adding that not doing so was "one of our mistakes." However, she felt it was "not easy to change it" as that would cause "tremendous dislocation."[81]

Mrs Gandhi's disdain for education and other human development and social security measures soon began to show in her government's budgetary allocations. Contrary to her rhetoric about caring for the wellbeing of the Indian people, her actions suggested that welfare was way down in her list of priorities. Her government's spending on these heads declined from 6.3 percent in 1969–70 to a little more than 5 percent during and after Emergency.

In his book *The Dynasty*, Gill vividly described what the Indian ruling establishment might consider the subversive potential of mass education—and therefore something to be wary of. He highlighted a report from the *Indian Express*, dated September 9, 1992, where "the Raigarh collector was suddenly transferred in spite of the fact that he was doing really good work in motivating people to attend the literary classes..." His colleague, the Collector of Durg, who was doing similarly good work, was also transferred. The reason turned out to be political and economic. The success of the literacy programme had made large farmers of the district fearful that if the campaign reached its logical conclusion, they would lose access to cheap and docile labour.[82]

Another report in the *Economic and Political Weekly*, dated November 21, 1992, described how women beneficiaries of the National Literary Mission in Nellore in Andhra Pradesh were inspired by a lesson on how women in a village, upset at the youth squandering all their money on arrack, mobilised the people to shut down the local arrack shops. Taking a cue from this story, the women decided to forcibly close down local arrack shops and stop the auction of liquor. This innocuous act began to threaten the powers that be. The sale of arrack accounted for a large part of the state's revenues and the women's agitation threatened to derail the state's budget. In addition, the big arrack contractors in the district were all influential Congressmen, and, therefore, their complaints against the agitation that was threatening their business got a patient hearing at the highest levels of the state government. The Chief Minister was upset at "some of the materials in the publications brought out in the literary missions." These, he warned, were not in sync with government policies and so would have to be expunged.[83] In 2016, the World Economic Forum (WEF) ranked India 104 out of 140 countries on the quality of its school education.

Literacy levels and enrolment figures have gone up significantly over the last few decades, but the same cannot be said about the quality of education being imparted to Indian students. In fact, it has earned the dubious honour of performing consistently poorly on this count. In 2012, Indian students ranked 72nd out of 73 countries globally in terms of learning outcomes based on Organisation for Economic Co-operation and Development (OECD) Secretariat's Programme for International Student Assessment (PISA). All of the East Asian countries—Singapore, Japan, Taiwan, Vietnam, and China—not only outperformed India but also emerged on the top of the rankings. Rather than prodding authorities in India to swing into action and make amends, the institutional response has been to boycott all PISA rankings after 2012.

The gross enrolment ratio for primary education has also increased over the years, indicating that more children are attending school. According to the District Information

System for Education 2019–20, the overall GER at the primary level was 99.8 percent. A report by the Azim Premji Foundation titled "Status of Learning Achievements in India: A Review of Empirical Research," however, found that despite the high enrolment rate, learning outcomes are poor and the dropout rate is alarmingly high:

> The fact that children are not learning is also evident from the dropping enrolment scenario, there being 30.5 million children in Class I and only 3.5 million in Class XII. The dropping enrolment reflects low learning in the system since most children are not completing grades for which they are enrolled…
>
> Even though children progress in primary grades due to the non-detention policy, in practice, little learning is taking place. Children are pushed from one grade to the next, irrespective of how much they are learning. Findings from a number of studies reveal that Class III/IV children are not able to read and write even simple sentences. Thus, something is surely wrong with the learning outcomes of children…
>
> Another factor contributing to the declining learning levels in schools is the curriculum load at each level, which makes it difficult for children to cope with the increasing quantity of facts and information. This has encouraged students to go in for private tuitions. A heavy curriculum works against first generation learners coming from poor backgrounds, who neither receive academic support at home nor can afford tuitions. As a result of the curriculum load, schools have lost sight of kindling creativity, developing a critical mindset in children, and inculcating a value system based on our Constitution.[84]

Though these examples are all from the post-Nehru, post-Indira periods, the political signals emanating from them were just as relevant and binding during their reigns. Nehru, in particular, was in complete denial of the failure of his dream to educate the Indian masses. The literacy rate for adults had crept up from 18 percent in 1951 to 28 percent in 1961. The female literacy rate had risen, if it can be called that, from a measly 8 percent in 1951 to an equally miserable 16 percent a decade later. But Nehru seemed unaware of the reality around him. "Education is spreading fairly well and today we have some fifty million boys and girls in our schools and colleges," he said.[85] And in a letter to Bernard Hollowood, English author and Editor of *Punch*, dated May 22, 1959, he wrote: "Already I see major changes taking place which are not perhaps so evident to outsiders... Probably the biggest revolution that is taking place in India is through women's education which affects directly the home."[86]

The 1985 Ministry of Education report titled *Challenge of Education*, rightly pointed out: "Many studies have shown that in the field of education, investments in elementary education yield the highest rate of returns and have a significant impact on productivity and general well-being of the masses." This was the great failure of the Indian education system.

Nehru's Vanity Blinded Him to Reality

Was Nehru blind to the reality of India after more than a decade of his rule? Or was he misinformed? Or was he being deliberately disingenuous? Though his biographers are silent on this aspect of his personality, several people close to him found him vain and conceited. Maulana Abul

Kalam Azad, his friend and associate who had the chance to observe him from very close quarters, said: "Jawaharlal is very vain and cannot stand that anybody else should receive greater support and admiration than he."[87] Rajkumari Amrit Kaur, Health Minister from 1947–57 and Kapurthala princess, who worked closely with Nehru for many years before and after Independence observed: "He is not averse to flattery and there is conceit in him which makes him at once intolerant of criticism and may even warp his better judgment."[88]

Azad and Kaur were two of Nehru's closest colleagues and their frank and blunt, view of his personality should not be ignored. It is possible that Nehru's conceit and arrogance came in the way of his accepting that his education policy, such as it was, had failed miserably to address the needs of India's population. It must have been even more galling for him to read about the success of education programmes in East and Southeast Asian countries. Denial and a deliberate downplaying of unfavourable outcomes seem to be the only plausible explanations, given that Nehru was presiding over a vast democratic apparatus and several important organs of state as well some global bodies had begun to flag the mess in the country's education system.

IITs Give India Hope

Even as the new Government of India's education policy was making it impossible for the vast majority of the country to access basic education, Nehruvian planners were laying the foundation for a new plutocracy that would create a thin sliver of well-educated people who would come to dominate India's intellectual, academic, administrative and corporate life over the next seven decades. Below this level were hundreds of millions of people with rudimentary or no education who eke out an existence as daily wagers, migrant workers, and similar lowly paid jobs at the margins of society.

Even as Nehruvian planners had no idea how to educate and empower the common people, they were looking ahead at how to improve the penetration of science and technology in the country. In 1950, the government set up the first IIT or Indian Institute of Technology at Kharagpur in West Bengal. A total of 210 students were admitted in the first batch. The plan was to increase admissions to 1,320 over the next five years. Four more IITs would be opened during Nehru's rule in Delhi, Mumbai, Kanpur, and Chennai. This was a pioneering and visionary move.

Over the decades, these institutes of higher education have become arguably the best-known Indian brands globally and have contributed significantly to India emerging as the world's IT capital. These institutes have gained global acclaim for being the alma mater of CEOs like Sundar Pichai of Alphabet, Vinod Khosla of Sun Microsystems, and Arvind Krishna of IBM, among several others. The IITs also played a major role in placing India at the centre of the global knowledge economy. For this, we have to thank the vision and prescience of India's first Prime Minister and his fascination with science.

But it is equally true that below the level of the IITs and a few other institutions of higher education, the quality of pedagogy begins to fall away rather precipitously. In a country as vast and populous as India, IIT graduates and their peers from other institutes form a minuscule minority that is smaller than the proverbial drop in the ocean.

The spread of primary education to every nook and corner of the country, to every village and to every locality would have helped reduce the huge disparities in the Indian society. The failure of the government on this count had precisely the opposite effect—it spread inequality and created two distinct classes of people. A tiny section of children mainly in the big cities went to English medium schools run by missionaries or by private trusts and business houses. They had access to the best education and opportunities. From these schools, students went to the IITs, the best liberal arts colleges, or medical colleges. Some of them went on to become civil servants, others became corporate leaders, yet others leading academics. A significant number of these students also went abroad for higher studies, causing a massive brain drain, denying the country the benefit of their intellect. Investments in these higher education institutes, almost all of them publicly run, left little money for the more important investments in primary schools.

Below this creamy layer and their elite schools and colleges were the government schools often with no blackboards, tables and chairs, where teachers were often absent, and which did not even have books for the students. Here, dropout rates were high and learning outcomes were abysmally poor.

Many experts have attempted to justify the low investment in primary education citing the scarcity of funding. This argument falls flat on its face when it is juxtaposed with the fast growth and consistent high investment in higher education in which the elite—which made these decisions—had a personal stake. If poor children started attending schools and then went for higher studies, businesses would have lost access to a cheap source of labour, the supply of cheap and subservient domestic helps would have been hit, and the government would have had to divert funding from higher education to primary schooling. Mahatma Gandhi, with his puckish sense of humour and his ability to succinctly sum up complex issues in short, easy-to-understand phrases, rightly said the heart of India's problem lay in the heartlessness of educated people.[89]

Elite Bias Creates India Versus Bharat Divide

The IITs, the IIMs and the high-profile focus on science and technology were in line with and complementary to Nehru's Temples of Modern India strategy, which privileged headline-grabbing programmes that benefited only a handful of people over less grandiose schemes that could have advanced the cause of people at the grassroots level. It is also possible that the high visibility and the buzz about this strategy sat very well with Nehru's sense of vanity.

The law of unintended consequences then began to kick in. Over the decades, the government's neglect of primary education and its elitist bias—as seen by the disproportionate focus on IITs, IIMs, higher education, and English—created a new fault line in the country: the much talked about India versus Bharat divide. Result: a thin sliver of well-educated but deracinated English-speaking elite emerged as the de facto ruling class, presiding over vast masses of semi-literate or illiterate people.

Macaulay's statement and vision found expression in full measure in Nehru's India.

> I feel… it is impossible for us… to attempt to educate the body of the people. We must at present do our best to form a class who may be interpreters between us and the millions whom we govern; a class of persons Indian in blood and colour, but English in tastes, in opinions, in morals, and in intellect.[90]

It is not clear when the phrase India versus Bharat was first coined, but its meaning is crystal clear. India, incorrectly seen as representing the tiny English-educated elite, was where the urbanised, economically advanced and socially progressive population lived. Bharat was home to the large mass of vernacular-educated or semi-literate or illiterate Indians, and was defined as primitive, inaccessible, and backward. It is also used to definitionally differentiate between those whose worldviews are informed by Western culture, ethics and sensibilities and those who adhere to traditional Indian values. So, in that sense, it is not necessarily a stark urban–rural divide. Parts of India and Bharat co-exist in every part of the country. Sharad Joshi, the farmer leader, wrote in *Business Line* in 2003:

> India is a notional entity, largely Anglicised and relatively better-off, which obtained the legacy of colonial exploitation from the British; while Bharat is largely rural, agricultural, poor and backward, and is subjected to colonial-like exploitation even after the end of the Raj.[91]

The divide is mainly cultural. The hegemony of the cosmopolitan, Anglicised elite, which had come to occupy pride of place in India's administrative, social and cultural life during the British Raj, not only continued but was cast in stone during the rule of Nehru and his successors. Over time, this elite emerged as the gatekeepers of Indian public discourse and the primary disseminator of knowledge. Their biases and prejudices crept into public policy, which was often detached from the lived experience of people in more indigenous settings. The social distance between the two groups is compounded by the condescending attitude of the former towards their provincial cousins. This is the lived experience of large sections of the people.

India's education system is very strange in that sense—the more people are educated the more they get alienated from their roots. It is this failing of the education system that has given rise to the feeling that Westernisation equals modernity and Indian traditions are a sign of backwardness.

For validation, dear reader, if you are part of the English medium-educated elite, take this test. Place your hand on your heart and ask yourself: Do you not look askance at your colleague who speaks broken English with a distinctly provincial accent? Do you not snigger at the person who goes to a posh restaurant and eats rice with his fingers? And do you not feel an instant connect with the client who speaks English with the same accent as yours, who uses the same idiom to communicate concepts, and whose worldviews are coloured by the same influences as you? And if you are a denizen of Bharat, have you not experienced subtle and not-so-subtle discrimination at the hands of the people in the above group?

There can be no doubt that Nehru would have been horrified had he lived to see the outcome of his education policy. There can also be very little debate that those policies were directly responsible for the creation of this chasm that shows no signs of being bridged. If you happen to say ancient India gave the world anything scientific—with the exception of the zero—like decimals, negative numbers, the calculation of pi, heliocentrism, or roundness of the earth, you will be laughed at and met with a rolling of eyes. Unfortunately, this policy has made the country—which is the world's largest democracy and also its birthplace—a quasi-plutocracy, where the vast masses of people residing in the proverbial Bharat have been denied their dues by the country's Western-educated elite.

How Lack of Education Affected Other Development Goals

At the time of Independence, the government had several priorities. Among them, rapid industrialisation, employment generation, improving agricultural productivity, population control and reducing and eliminating caste discrimination hinged on another equally important but sadly neglected priority—education.

As noted above, universal female education not only helped East Asian countries industrialise rapidly, but it also reduced fertility rates and led to an improvement in child health as they delayed marriage and had fewer children. Another social ill that education addressed in these countries was the eradication of the "son preference" which resulted in a larger count of boys at birth.

Then, education was also expected to loosen the stranglehold of caste, especially in rural India, by reordering the economic relations between various social groups. But the government's failure to spread primary education throughout the length and breadth of the country precluded the possibility of enlightenment becoming the harbinger of social engineering in India.

India grew at 3.6 percent during the 1951–80 period. This was much slower than the growth rate achieved by the East Asian Tigers, although it was a huge improvement over the stagnation under British Rule in the first half of the twentieth century. However, even this relatively tardy pace of economic growth was considerably offset by population growth of 2.0–2.3 percent.[92] As a result, the benefits of economic growth did not show up in improved standards for the people.

Sector Denied Adequate Funding

The above goals could have been achieved only if the government put its cheque book where its rhetoric was and allocated sufficient funds for education. However, Nehru's administration spent only about 2 percent of GDP on education against the figure of 4–6 percent recommended by experts.[93]

Expenditure on primary education has a direct relationship with development, and this proposition is validated by examples from within India itself. In the mid-1960s, Kerala was spending twice as much per primary school student as Uttar Pradesh was. No surprise then that it had more schools, better teachers and a tradition of serving free lunches. Result: more children completed schooling in Kerala than in Uttar Pradesh, giving the former a literacy rate of 70 percent in 1970 compared to 22 percent in the latter.[94] This had a positive spin-off mirroring the experience of East and Southeast Asia. Better primary and secondary education created higher social awareness, and this prompted the government to put in place better health facilities.[95] Uttar Pradesh, on the other hand, continued to lag far behind.

The Report Card

In 1951, the first census after Independence estimated India's population at 361 million and literacy rate at 18.33 percent.[96] That means 295 million people were illiterate. In 1991, only about 52 percent of India's population of 830 million was literate. That means about 400 million Indians were illiterate. In four and a half decades of Independence, most of it ruled by Nehru, his daughter and his grandson, the population of illiterate people had actually increased by a third.

Education outcomes at the end of Nehru's rule and in 1984 when Indira Gandhi was assassinated make for dismal reading. The literacy rate, which was at about 16 percent in 1947, crept up to 28 percent in 1961 according to the Census of that year, which is the closest to 1964 when Nehru passed away. Given a population of about 480 million then, the number of unlettered people in India was in the range of 340 million. In 1991, when the Nehruvian development model was finally jettisoned, India's literacy rate was at 52 percent. The figures for males and females were at 63.9 percent and 39.4 percent, respectively. For an apples-to-apples comparison, China, which started from a similar level as India in the late 1940s, had achieved a literacy rate of 77.79 percent in 1990.[97] Taiwan and South Korea, both of which began their respective development journeys much after 1947, i.e. after India began hers, had literacy rates in the range of 90 percent, according to World Population Review.

Look at the way Singapore's visionary leader Lee Kew Yuan tackled the problem. Instead of being overwhelmed by the gargantuan crises confronting the newly independent city state after its separation from the Malaysian Federation in 1965—being left to fend for itself with no natural resources and little prospects for the future—Lee began investing in his people. He did not complain, as Nehru did to his sister that "we live here from crisis to crisis and all planning has been postponed."[98] Making the best of a difficult situation, Lee tried to compensate for the absence of natural resources by investing in his people. Commenting on this aspect of Singapore's development, former Prime Minister Goh Chok Tong said in March 1997 that the city state was "blessed" by the lack of natural resources; this left it with no choice but to develop its greatest asset—its people.[99]

Unlike India, which invested in the so-called temples of modern India while neglecting the laity, Lee treated education as a "national investment." There was a 200-fold increase in the expenditure on education between 1959 and 2000. As a consequence of this far-sighted approach, the literacy rate improved from 72.2 percent in 1970 to 97 percent in 2016.[100]

Japan, too, owes much of its global economic dominance to the success of its primary and secondary education programme. American academic William Lockwood, in his book *The Economic Development of Japan*, described how Japan transformed itself from an agrarian society into one of the world's foremost industrialised societies. He observed:

> The mass of people never got beyond six years' schooling. But even this helped to diffuse the more modest technical skills widely among the population, especially in the

> towns and cities. And education encouraged an increasing degree of geographic, occupational, and social mobility among the people, which was essential to the radical restructuring of the economy. Finally, by spreading economic opportunity without legal discrimination with relation to race, religion, or class, it was the chief force at work, however ineffectively, to combat the great inequality so deeply rooted in Japanese society. No other enterprise of the state paid handsome dividends to the nation.[101]

Nehru, unfortunately, did not draw any lessons from this example. The track record of the Government of India on education and literacy in the first 44 years of Independence, thus, was poor when compared to peer nations in Asia. At no time after the end of the First Plan period did the Nehru government make universal primary education its overweening priority. Far from it. Indira Gandhi openly declared her lack of interest in universal primary education as a goal worthy of pursuing. These two Prime Ministers ruled for a combined 33 years, and so had a disproportionate influence on the hits and misses of the period under review. Rajiv Gandhi ruled India for a further five years but that was too short a period to make any decisive breakthroughs in this critical sphere.

Although Indira Gandhi admitted in passing that Nehru had made a mistake by not focusing his administrative attention and budgetary allocations toward education, she made no effort to mitigate this neglect and after that one admission of mistake did not mention this issue again. In his five years as Prime Minister, Rajiv Gandhi did not announce any major policy or budgetary intervention in favour of primary education. There was no significant improvement in outcomes in this field, either. The other governments that ruled India during this period—of Lal Bahadur Shastri, Morarji Desai, Charan Singh, V.P. Singh, and Chandrasekhar—did not last long enough to make any significant difference to the education policy of the government. But as Indira Gandhi admitted, Nehru's neglect of primary education made it difficult for successor governments to play catch up. So, his government must bear a disproportionate share of the responsibility for the poor state of education in India today and the consequent backwardness of large swathes of the Indian population.

Commenting on Nehru, noted historian Ramachandra Guha told Dilip Thakore of EducationWorld in an interview:

> ...coming to Nehru himself, he had enormous achievements and enormous failures. Contrary to those who think that the Soviet model of economics was his greatest failure, I believe his greatest failure—and this is relevant to your magazine—was to ignore primary education. He didn't recognise that in a true democracy the first priority should be to remove illiteracy.[102]

5

Government Fails the Farmers

Agriculture was the dominant sector of the Indian economy in 1947. It accounted for more than 55 percent of the GDP and about 75 percent of employment at the time of Independence.[103] Any programme to uplift the Indian masses and its economy would have to focus on improving the lot of the Indian agricultural sector. No wonder Mahatma Gandhi said that India lives in its villages.

But two centuries of neglect under the colonial British Government, rampant exploitation of tenant-farmers by landlords and *zamindars*, absence of investments in the sector, outdated farming practices, and lack of access to cheap credit, scientific techniques and high yielding seeds had combined to stifle the prospects of this important segment of the Indian economy.

But there was hope in the air. Indian farmers needed a booster dose of investments and technology infusion to kick start a revival that would lift them out of their moribund existence. The new Government of India, led by the progressive Prime Minister Jawaharlal Nehru and armed with a new scientific temper, seemed poised to do just that.

It made a good start. The First Five Year Plan (1951–56) rightly focused on developing agriculture and irrigation and allocated Rs. 601 crore or 31 percent of the planned investment of Rs. 1,960 crore to these heads.[104] The government managed to reclaim about 12 lakh acres of land and brought this under farming. Another 14 million acres were brought under irrigation, and the Japanese method of intensive rice cultivation, which improved yields and reduced wastage, was introduced in large parts of the country.

The outcomes were very encouraging. The country achieved self-sufficiency in food, the price index for farm commodities (1952–53 = 100) fell to 92.8 as food grains, sugarcane, cotton and oilseeds exceeded the targeted increase in production by 1.0–4.2 percent. Only jute output recorded a 12 percent decline, but that was primarily because the primary jute producing areas had gone to East Pakistan, thus, depriving India of vast jute growing areas.[105]

The First Plan was a success, and this prompted the planners to set more ambitious targets in the Second Five Year Plan. But this was when Nehru turned his attention to the development of heavy industries and took his eyes off agriculture. Allocation fell to 20 percent of the Plan expenditure and the government's focus shifted to industry. This meant that the government could not address the problem of unemployment and disguised unemployment, especially in rural India by creating low skilled jobs in small and medium enterprises that would draw excess labour away from India's farms and into the nascent but more productive industrial sector.[106]

The success of agriculture under the First Five Year Plan hid several systemic weaknesses, policy loopholes and administrative shortcomings that would continue to hobble this sector for decades to come. The biggest of these shortcomings was the failure of land reforms and the Nehru government's connivance with Congress' support base among rich landlords and powerful middlemen in ensuring that the gains from redistribution of land remained confined mostly to official documents and reports.

The First Five Year Plan had recognised this problem. "The future of land ownership and cultivation constitutes perhaps the most fundamental issue in national development. To a large extent, the pattern of economic and social organisation will depend upon the manner in which the land problem is resolved," the Plan clearly said.[107]

In rural India, power and influence is exercised by those who own and control land and its produce. In many cases, this ownership and influence was a direct consequence of British rule. In order to ensure the collection of revenues from the hinterland of Bengal, British Governor General Lord Cornwallis introduced the Permanent Settlement in 1793, which created a class of middlemen called *zamindars* who were given ownership of vast tracts of lands in perpetuity in return for rents to the "Company Bahadur" (government run by the East India Company). Within a few decades, this system was introduced in other parts of the country with some regional variations.

This class of people continued to exercise tremendous influence even after Independence and formed the bulk of the middle-rung leadership of the Congress party, especially outside the big cities and towns. The class interest of this group and its instincts of self-preservation successfully saw off Nehru's initial enthusiasm for land reforms.

Lessons Not Learnt from Japan

There were examples abroad that India could have followed. In 1949, Nehru wrote to the Prime Ministers (as chief ministers were called before India became a republic) of the provinces, highlighting the "relatively short period of time" in which Japan had achieved "astonishing development." As in the field of education, where the example set by Japan was followed a few years later by other nations in East and Southeast Asia, India did not learn the right lessons from its Asian peers. For example,

> land reform in 1949 actually provided a foundation for equitable development in [South] Korea. For instance, between 1947 and 1964, tenant farmers fell from 42 percent of the total farm households to a mere 5 percent, while tiller-owners increased from 16.5 percent to 72 percent...[108]

This showed the success of land reforms initiated in the late 1940s, around the same time as India embarked on the same journey. But, unlike in India, "the land was fairly evenly distributed to the farmers and absentee land owners and large-scale land holders were virtually eliminated."[109]

This was not the only point of departure from the Indian development model. "The Korean model is not that of industrialisation only at the expense of all other areas. For instance, despite the priority accorded to industrial development, the agricultural sector" was not

> totally ignored. In fact, there were periods, in particular, during the earlier part of the 1970s when agriculture came to the fore of development strategy. By and large, the goal of governmental policies has been avoidance of an excessive

> urban-rural disparity in income. The fairly equitable pattern of income distribution that emerged from the earlier success in land reform obviated much of the policymakers' concern with distributional issues in implementing rapid growth strategies. The Korean government did not have to spend a large amount of its budget for social welfare and could concentrate its limited resources on high-growth sectors of the economy.[110]

South Korea up to well into the 1960s truly represented a backward, desolate economy based on subsistence agriculture"—much like India at that time. It is about the size of Kerala and smaller than Haryana. Interestingly,

> unlike the northern part of the peninsula, South Korea is poor in natural resources. Only about 30 percent of the land area is cultivable and the arable land per farm household ranks among the lowest in the world. Korean society was traditional, feudalistic, agrarian, and isolated… until the late nineteenth century.[111]

If this provided a template for Indian planners in the 1960s and 1970s, Japan had earlier set benchmarks that Indian planners considered achievable. Between 1880 and 1920, Japan managed to double the productivity of its farm workers. Grain output increased 77 percent even as the number of farm workers actually fell over these four decades and the area under cultivation increased 20 percent.[112]

The First Plan recognised that Indian farms had productivity levels that were only about 20 percent of Japanese farms. It also noted that Japan had achieved massive productivity gains "mainly through better seeds, manure, and insecticides, and improved agricultural practices, none of which required large capital outlays." To improve their productivity, Indian farms needed to catch up with Japanese levels, and, for this to happen, land reforms was seen as *sine qua non*. To meet the goal of higher productivity, Indian farmers also needed more extension services—technical support services to help farming activities.[113]

Regarding South Korea's post-Korean War economic development, historian Michael J. Seth noted:

> South Korea's economic transformation was also made possible by the social transformation that was occurring in the country at this time... In particular, two fundamental changes in South Korea contributed enormously to the country's eventual economic take-off. One was land reform, a crucial element in South Korea's economic as well as social modernization. Korea was a predominantly rural peasant society in 1945 still dominated by descendants of the old *yangban* landholding aristocratic class; the majority of farmers owned little or no land. Land reform was an emotionally charged issue. The South Korean government, dominated by conservative members of the landowning class, was reluctant to carry out land reform. But worried by the influence of North Korea... the National Assembly passed a land reform act in 1949. ... Under the land reform, property holdings were limited to 7.5 acres; farmers receiving redistributed acreage had to pay 150 percent of the annual value of the land received over a ten-year period. While this initially left them with a large debt, the high rate of inflation made it easy to pay off. The result was dramatic; in 1944, 3 percent of landowners owned 64 percent of the farmland; but in 1956, the top 6 percent of landowners owned only 18 percent, and tenancy had virtually disappeared.

Few developments changed South Korea so profoundly, so quickly. Traditional peasants became small entrepreneurial farmers. The conservative landlords, rather than disappearing completely, now directed their capital and energy toward business or education. Since the 1910s, some members of the landed aristocracy had been entering business; the land reform accelerated this trend. Many others established private schools, universities, and private educational foundations. In this way, land reforms contributed to the foundations of a prosperous society. It brought stability to the countryside and redirected much of the capital and entrepreneurial energy of the old landlord class toward commerce, industry, and education.[114]

Why Land Reforms Failed

Some of these developments admittedly took place after the initial Indian experiment with land reforms, but, like the Nehru government, the South Korean administration too did not have a readymade template to follow and had to chart its own path as it went along. That it managed to overcome the vested interests and the other challenges that stymied the Indian programme is a testament to better plan architecture, pragmatic political management and more efficient implementation.

In India, the farmer had to be given security of tenure and, better still, ownership of the land he tilled. For this, *zamindari* had to be abolished. In his usual lofty, rhetorical style Nehru wrote to the state chief ministers that if *zamindari* abolition fails "our entire social and economic policy fails."

Although *zamindari* was duly abolished via legislation, several loopholes in the law—as well as the class interests of those in charge of implementing the devolution of land ownership and the underlying land relations that had sustained the system for almost two centuries—proved more difficult to uproot and continues to hinder the delivery of social justice to this day.

Several large tenant farmers found themselves as owners of the land they tilled and this created a new class of prosperous farmers who, over time, emerged as a special interest group that cornered a disproportionate share of the benefits earmarked for farmers for themselves.

Then, many tenants could not prove their tenancy in the absence of proper land records and the practice in many parts of the country of oral tenancy rights. This allowed *zamindars* to evict such tenants by claiming that the land was self-cultivated and that these lands were, in effect, home farms. They did not have to physically cultivate the land themselves. Mere supervision qualified them for this concession.

Obviously, those in charge of drawing up the new laws were less interested in social equity than the political rhetoric seemed to suggest.[115] Then, long-drawn litigation between a section of *zamindars* and the states gave the former enough time to change the land records and illegally register the land in the names of relatives, associates, even pets, and other *benami* name lenders. This allowed the *zamindars* to retain effective control of the land and defeat the intent of the progressive legislation enacted by the government.

Nehru again showed his unwillingness to get into the granular details of policy implementation and admitted in a letter to chief ministers that "this result has not been what we had looked forward to."[116]

The other pillar of Nehru's plan to revitalise Indian agriculture—extension services—also failed miserably. Red tape and bureaucratic controls came in the way of efficient implementation of these services. Those in charge of actual work on the ground lacked knowledge and training and farmers refused to heed their advice.[117]

But the main problem, Theodore Shultz, Professor of Economics at the University of Chicago said, was that Indian farmers were "generally illiterate." They also had "low levels of skills." What they needed was more than a "strong back" and the stamina for hard "manual labour." Japanese farm workers, on the other hand, armed with primary and sometimes secondary school education, found it easier to carry out complex and difficult farm practices and absorb lessons imparted by well-trained extension workers.

Lack of Grassroots Connect

One big reason for the failure of Nehru's land reforms was its formulation and implementation by his advisors and civil servants, none of whom had any first-hand experience or knowledge of farming. This had to do, probably, with his comfort levels with people from his own social and educational background (as discussed in Chapter 4), his poor opinion of Indian farmers, and his chronic reluctance to let ground-level data influence his thinking. An issue as important and sensitive as land reforms should have been planned as a mass movement, with the participation of ground-level Congress workers who should have primed the intended beneficiaries about the possibilities as well as their rights, entitlements and duties. A vast majority of them were illiterate and too timid to take on the might of the *zamindars* and big landowners who controlled all the economic and social levers in the villages. If, instead of just the government servants, local Congress workers, who were aware of the unique situations in each village and block, had been involved in the process of land reforms, the programme could have had a better chance of success.

However, the land reforms programme initiated by Nehru did have some achievements to its credit. For one, by abolishing the institution of *zamindari*, it freed many tenant farmers from the yoke of feudal exploitation. It also led to lower rents and brought to an end the imposition of several other levies and taxes that *zamindars* would extract from peasants for their own benefit. With their feudal masters passing into history, as many as 20 million peasants gained ownership rights over the *zamindari* estates that they had cultivated for generations. These brought considerable relief to millions of farmers.

But the failure of the programme left many more losers in its wake. Several million small farmers, who could not prove their tenancy in the absence of written contracts, lost their rights and were reduced to the status of landless poor.

Indira Gandhi did try to remedy the situation as part of her *Garibi Hatao* programme, but, like most of her other programmes, this one, too, was marked by tokenism and shoddy implementation. Also, like her father, she seemed more interested in garnering laudatory headlines than in actually making a difference on the ground. Using the government's special emergency powers, Indira Gandhi confiscated 1.1 million acres of excess land from large farmers and redistributed it to poor and landless tillers to the accompaniment of fawning reports and adulatory public discourse.

But did this really make a significant difference to the lives of Indian farmers as a community? The short but brutal answer to that will have to be a resounding "No"! The land that was redistributed was only about a quarter percent of the total cultivated land area of 400 million acres, and this record was only marginally better than the rate that her father's government had achieved.[118] The approach to and the implementation of land reforms followed a top-down model that was destined to fail. The picture could well have been different if Nehru and Indira had got block-level Congress workers involved in the process rather than depending on civil servants and other government employees with no skin in the game and little knowledge of the issues at hand.

The Origins of Vote Bank Politics

Indian politicians have always depended on wealthy backers for funding and other resources. In the early days of the republic, the Congress was especially dependent on the largesse and goodwill of the landed gentry, both for funding and their large vote banks. This made the implementation of the land reforms programme difficult. The abolition of *zamindari* did not bring about too radical a change in rural socio-political equations.

With the *zamindars* gone, a new class of prosperous farmers, whom some analysts have dubbed capitalist farmers, emerged. They have, over the decades, become a special interest group with political clout out of proportion to their size. Their demands sometimes pit them against their urban counterparts and is another manifestation of the urban–rural divide that we discussed in Chapter 4. As this class of capitalist farmers gained political influence, its class interests—which was decisively ranged against radical land reforms and any large-scale redistribution of agricultural land—came in the way of a wholesale reordering of rural socio-economic relationships, which was necessary to reform and modernise the agriculture sector.

That India was not ready for radical land reforms became clear when powerful state-level leaders joined forces to scuttle Nehru's progressive policy intervention. To be sure, few frontline leaders openly opposed land reforms but when it came to implementing it in villages and blocks, there was a definite waning in the enthusiasm of the political leadership, which placed roadblocks in its way. Several chief ministers, who depended on rural landed interests for their vote banks, also intervened on behalf of their political benefactors and applied pressure on the Centre to slow down. With right wing parties snooping around for a political opening, they were wary of ceding ground and the support of these important electoral intermediaries.[119]

Nehru, who was enamoured of the Soviet model of development, the primacy of the public sector and industrialisation led by heavy industries, had only a limited understanding of the dynamics of the multi-layered rural relationships that informed India's agricultural economy. Perhaps because of this, he did not organise any mass movement to mobilise the peasantry and raise their social awareness, which could have prepared the ground for the redistribution of land that followed.[120]

However, as was his wont, instead of looking within and questioning the basis of his policy choices and their shoddy implementation for the failure of his agricultural policy, Nehru tried to shift the blame to "bad harvests" and the ways of Indian farmers who remained steeped in "orthodoxy and old customs."[121]

But, in the end, he had to give up the pretence. "Indeed, it has become rather a joke in some foreign countries when they refer to land reforms in India. We have talked tall and done nothing," he wrote in a letter.[122]

Second and Third Plan Failures

The success of the First Plan, especially in the agriculture sector, lulled the planners into a false sense of complacence. Nehru and his advisors thought that they had solved the country's farming problems and, hence, could now focus on the Prime Minister's new pet fetish—heavy industries, encapsulated in the "Temples of Modern India" policy. The Plan outlay on the farm sector was cut down from 31 percent to 20 percent, although, in monetary terms, the allocation at Rs 1,050 crore was higher. The optimism about the prospects of this sector prompted the planners to revise upwards the targets set for various crops in the Second Plan using the same measures that had been used in the First.

The government's change of priorities, from farming to industry, showed in the outcomes. The total area under irrigation increased 16 million acres compared to the target of 21 million acres. Fertiliser consumption also increased at a tardy pace, much slower than envisaged in the Plan. The overall output of most crops—food grains, oilseeds, cotton, and jute—fell short of their targets by between 1.0 percent and 1.8 percent. Only sugarcane and tea production overshot their Plan targets.

The shortfall in food production led to a rise in prices and fuelled inflation, hurting the overall economy.[123] The wholesale price index soared a worrying 35 percent during the Plan period and set off a chain of other economic problems. The most damaging of these was the cascading effect of the rise in farm prices on the prices of other commodities. The shortfall in food production, coupled with the rise in prices, forced the government to resume the import of food grains, which had been cut during the First Five Year Plan. With the export-shy industrial policy not generating any new sources of foreign exchange earnings, this meant that precious foreign currency that had been set aside for the import of plant and machinery and other industrial raw materials had to be diverted for the import of food.

The Plan architecture was directly responsible for this, and Nehru and the Plan's author Prashanta Chandra Mahalanobis, despite the huge political capital and academic brilliance that they brought to the exercise, must bear responsibility for this.

The Third Five Year Plan (1961–66) fared no better. Drawing the right lessons from the failure of the Second Plan, the Nehru government set out to achieve the twin targets of attaining self-sufficiency in food grains and increase the exports of farm produce. The Plan clearly stated that agriculture was the first priority of the government's development agenda. The planners were by now aware, on the basis of experience gained from the first two plans, that the rate of growth of farm production was one of the main factors limiting the growth of the Indian economy.

It said in no uncertain terms that farm production had to be increased to the greatest extent possible and adequate provisions made to ensure funds were available to attain this goal. It also envisaged diversifying the rural economy and bringing down the proportion of rural people dependent of agriculture.

These were reasonable, practical goals, and no one can find any fault with the thinking behind this Plan. However, the implementation left much to be desired, and the funds allocated for it proved inadequate. Like the Second Plan, this one too failed and set the Indian agricultural sector and the overall economy back by several years.

The Plan targeted a food grains production increase of 30 percent, or an average growth of 6 percent per year. The actual growth over the five-year-period was 10 percent. That means that the growth crawled along at 2 percent per year, i.e. one-third the planned figure. Food grains output fell short of the Plan target by as much as 27.3 percent. The production of oilseeds, cotton and jute also fell short but by smaller margins of 3.7 percent, 2.3 percent and 1.7 percent, respectively. Of the major crops, only sugarcane overshot the targeted output by 1.8 percent during the Third Plan. The result was widespread shortages of food grains and other agricultural commodities and a spike in the prices of food.

The Index of food grain prices shot up from 118.4 in 1961–62 to 168.8 in 1965–66.[124] Far from increasing the export of food grains and farm output as per the Plan target, the government was forced to import food grains during the Plan period to overcome the food shortage and to feed the huge Indian population. This set the stage for India to go around the world with a begging bowl for food to feed its population and funds to keep its economy afloat.

How Charan Singh Stood up to Nehru and Saved India's Farmers

Today, Charan Singh, whose memory has been resurrected following the posthumous award of the Bharat Ratna by the Narendra Modi government, is a largely forgotten figure except in some pockets of Western Uttar Pradesh where his family continues to wield political influence. He is best known for succeeding Morarji Desai and becoming the fifth Prime Minister of India for a period of 23 days and also for being the only Prime Minister never to face the Parliament.

He is also well known for becoming the first non-Congress chief minister of Uttar Pradesh when he was elected to the post on April 3, 1967. Besides these two events, he is famous for being a renowned farmer leader who highlighted issues dear to farmers all his public life.

However, his greatest contribution to Indian farming, the country's economy and, indeed, its public life has been airbrushed out of history books. One reason for this could be the urban versus rural divide, where issues only of concern to the cosmopolitan elite find resonance in the public discourse. The other reason is more political. Because it showed Nehru in poor light, his descendants and followers, who controlled the public discourse and were in charge of disseminating information to the world at large for many years after his death, wiped out this part of India's history from the popular records of the time.

Nehru's India was experiencing the high noon of socialism in 1959. Just four years previously, at its Avadi session in 1955, the ruling Congress party had passed a resolution calling for a "socialist pattern" of society in India, and state control over the means of production was the presiding mantra of the times.

Having set India on the path of "socialist development" with the adoption of his "Temples of Modern India" strategy, which privileged heavy industries like steel plants and the large multi-purpose projects like the Bhakra Nangal dam over employment-generating but less glamorous development pathways like encouragement of wage goods, Nehru was keen on replicating the Soviet experiment in the Indian agricultural sector as well.

Grappling with low farm productivity and the repeated failure of the sector to meet Plan targets, Nehru wanted to adopt collectivisation as the panacea for the shortcomings plaguing this critical segment of the Indian economy and wanted the Congress to pass a resolution to this effect at its 1959 session in Nagpur. Though many farmer leaders were opposed to the idea, none of them had the political heft or the gumption to stand up to Nehru, then at the peak of his popularity and powers. Collective farming, which would involve taking away farms from individual farmers and subsuming them within larger farming collectives, would increase agricultural production and lift the farmers out of poverty, said Nehru and his followers. It was the zeitgeist of the times, and anyone who dared to oppose Nehru was dubbed a reactionary and an enemy of the farmers.

Collective farming was already a major failure in the Soviet Union and was causing millions of people untold tragedy, but this was being kept a carefully guarded secret from the rest of the world. For context, *Encyclopaedia Britannica* defines collectivisation as

> the policy adopted by the Soviet government, pursued most intensively between 1929 and 1933, to transform traditional agriculture in the Soviet Union and to reduce the economic power of the kulaks (prosperous peasants). Under collectivisation, the peasantry were forced to give up their individual farms and join large collective farms.[125]

The plan was an abject failure and led to untold human misery:

> Output fell, but the government, nevertheless, extracted the large amounts of agricultural produce it needed to acquire the capital for industrial investment. This caused a major famine in the countryside (1932–33) and the deaths of millions of peasants.

The same story also played out in China:

> In 1955, the Maoists speeded up the process of collectivisation. After this came the Great Leap Forward, a refinement of the traditional five-year plans and other efforts to mobilize the masses into producing small scale industries throughout China. The experiment's waste, confusion, and inefficient management combined with natural calamities to produce a prolonged famine (1959–61) that killed 15–30 million people.

This was the template that Nehru wanted to impose on the Indian farming community. Only one mid-ranking Congress functionary from Uttar Pradesh called Charan Singh opposed the resolution. In a hard hitting speech that lasted one hour, he held forth forcefully on why collective farming was "wholly unsuitable to Indian realities."

In his book *Joint Farming X-Rayed: The Problem and its Solution*, Singh explained why he opposed collectivisation. He wrote:

> Attachment to the land is a universal trait in all countries. The French peasant, for instance, calls his land his "mistress"...
>
> Human nature is the same everywhere. Here, our peasant calls his land his *Dharti Mata*—Mother Earth—inasmuch as it provides sustenance for all living things. Everywhere the peasant is a firm believer in property striving for independence. Hence, a collectivist economy will meet with his emotional resistance from the start. Ultimately, it is not a question of economic efficiency or of form of organization, but whether individualism or collectivism should prevail. Peasantry represents not only a certain form of economy but also a certain way of life. Within the peasantry, those characters, traits, and moral forces are most forced which resist the tendency towards collectivism and of being levelled down into a uniform mass.[126]

Charan Singh, thus, saved India from the prospect of mass starvation and a social and political tragedy that could have completely dislocated the lives of the 70 percent of Indians in the rural countryside, and, for this India, will have to remain eternally grateful to him. If it had not been for his courage of conviction, all the subsequent benefits that accrued from the Green Revolution that was launched a few years later might never have materialised. Then, the probable rural disruptions could have exacerbated and provided fuel to the Naxalite uprising that reared its head in some parts of the country in the late 1960s and taken the country down a very different path, which could have been very difficult to correct.

Participating in a parliamentary debate a few months before Nehru's death, Member of Parliament Dr B.N. Singh said:

> If you take a glimpse of rural India, you will see a more ghastly spectacle—indescribable poverty and misery in every village, a daily income of between 19 and 31 nP for over half of the population; population increase outstripping national income growth, illiteracy still between 70 to 80 per cent, caste's apartheid spreading within society like a fungus disease, an epidemic here and a famine there, corruption in the police, graft in government, cynicism and patronage in higher politics, bullying and intimidation in lower, gloom and frustration written large on the face of the people.[127]

Food Shortage, PL 480, and India's Ship-to-Mouth Existence

By the end of Nehru's rule, the optimism and hope that had marked the beginning of his term had given way to cynicism and despair. The back-to-back failures of the Second and Third Five Year Plans meant that the economy was beset with shortages of almost all items of day-to-day use. Food production had been stagnant for years and the expected industrial boom had not taken place. Industry had not delivered the benefits that Nehru had promised, and unemployment, already unacceptably high, was rising at an alarming pace. The average inflation rate in 1964 was at a high of 13.36 percent, bringing misery all round.[128]

Lal Bahadur Shastri, an unassuming man with grit and ability that belied his humble exterior, set about the task of repairing India's broken farm system that had largely been ignored by his larger-than-life predecessor. By this time, India was surviving on huge American wheat shipments, which had begun in the early 1950s and reached 4.3 million tonnes by 1963.[129]

These wheat shipments were the result of a combination of political exigency and hypocrisy in the US political economy. To keep its politically crucial farm lobby happy, the American government was paying a support price for wheat that was more than the market price. This left the US government with massive wheat stocks that it could not sell. The alternatives before it was to burn it, throw it into the sea or give it away to poor nations, since storing such a huge quantity of wheat entailed a significant cost that could not be recovered. The US Congress did not like these options. To get around this, the PL-480 law came to be enacted—to allow the sales of this wheat to developing countries in local currencies. B.K. Nehru, India's Ambassador to the US, wrote: "The representatives of the people had objected to giving away the taxpayer's money to foreigners. They had relented only when they were told that the proposal was not to give away anything but to sell it on credit."

It was these shipments that cemented India's image as a "basket case" that lived ship-to-mouth. But, despite living on the largesse of the US administration, India, especially after Indira Gandhi came to power in 1966, continued with its prickly, ideology-driven anti-US diplomatic rhetoric, completely oblivious to the humanitarian disaster it was courting if Washington turned off the wheat tap.

And turn off it, it did, at least once, probably to teach the Indian leadership a lesson. B.K. Nehru speculated that it could have been US President Lyndon B. Johnson's way of getting the message across that Washington had not appreciated the Indo–Soviet joint statement that had criticised the US actions in Vietnam.

Many Indians found the situation humiliating, but, in the absence of a revival in the farming sector, there was little they could do. And the farm sector, which continued to suffer the government's policy mistakes and administrative mismanagement, seemed in no position to deliver the growth that would allow India to become self-sufficient in food grains.

Green Revolution Solves India's Food Grains Crisis

Shastri, who inherited a country in crisis, decided to take the bull by the horns. His master stroke was to appoint Chidambaram Subramaniam as the Minister of Food and Agriculture. This single move changed India and had as far reaching an impact on the Indian economy and self-image as did the appointment of Dr Manmohan Singh to the role of the Finance Minister by P.V. Narasimha Rao almost three decades later.

In the 1940s, the Rockefeller Foundation began a collaboration with the Mexican government to develop new methods to boost wheat production. In 1944, Norman Borlaug joined the Cooperative Wheat Research Production Program team that had been assembled for the purpose and stayed for 16 years during which he developed several high-yield, disease resistant semi-dwarf wheat varieties. By 1963, 95 percent of Mexico's wheat crop used one of Borlaug's semi-dwarf varieties. By this time, Mexico, which had been grappling with shortages in 1944 when Borlaug joined the programme, had become self-sufficient and a net exporter of wheat.

In the early 1960s, some of these dwarf varieties of wheat were sent to the Indian Agricultural Research Institute at Pusa for testing. The test results were encouraging and, when reports of this experiment reached Subramaniam, events took on a life of their own. He realised that the report lying on his desk could hold the key to the holy grail of Indian agriculture—self-sufficiency in food grains production.

But several hurdles would have to be overcome before the potential of the pilot production at Pusa could be translated into the reality of bountiful harvests that would put an end to the humiliating spectre of Indians surviving on American dole. Overcoming great political resistance, and supported by a young agro-scientist M.S. Swaminathan and civil servant B. Sivaraman, he hired a fleet of Boeing 707 freighters and imported 16,000 tons of seeds of the new dwarf variety of wheat. He also convinced Shastri to use his political capital to use scarce foreign exchange to import massive quantities of fertilisers and also went against the conventional wisdom of the times by inviting multinational corporations to set up chemical fertiliser plants in India.

Through the entire process of chaperoning what came to be called the Green Revolution, Subramaniam fought a running battle with the then Finance Minister T.T. Krishnamachari, who opposed his proposal to raise wheat prices by 15 percent. But Subramaniam, with the full backing of Shastri, stood his ground. To be successful, the new wheat varieties would need sufficient supplies of fertilisers, remunerative prices, and assured availability of water. It would also require increased mechanisation and increased use of pesticides to protect the plants from insects and diseases. The experiment would fail if any of these inputs were taken away. All of these would need the government's unstinting support and the Prime Minister was determined to provide it, regardless of the opposition.

The new wheat variety was a huge gamble when Subramaniam bet on it, but the risks were worth the reward. Not only was a vocal section of the Indian establishment opposed to it, their scepticism was shared by many international experts also. In his 1968 book *The Population Bomb*, biologist and author Paul R. Ehlrich wrote:

> The battle to feed all of humanity is over. In the 1970s… hundreds of millions of people are going to starve to death in spite of any crash programs embarked upon now.[130] … I have yet to meet anyone familiar with the situation who thinks India will be self-sufficient in food by 1971, if ever.[131]

He added that India could not possibly "feed two hundred million more people by 1980."[132]

The book became a bestseller, but its calamitous forecast proved to be off the mark by a wide margin. After reaching a high of 8 million tons in 1966, India's wheat imports began to taper off as domestic production skyrocketed. After a brief spike in the mid-1970s, it came down to zero in 1979,[133] decisively disproving Ehlrich's dark forecast.

The Green Revolution has had several negative after-effects that are now becoming apparent. However, this is not the right forum to discuss them.

The "basket case" of the Nehru years now has wheat and rice stocks in excess of 50 million (500 lakh) metric tonnes and is a net exporter of both wheat and rice. PL-480 and phrases like "ship-to-mouth" are now a distant memory that many young Indians may not even be aware of. Swaminathan has rightly been called the Father of the Green Revolution and Subramaniam the Political Father of the Green Revolution. But the man who silently launched this revolution and gave it his political backing, without which it could have got derailed, was Shastri. Unfortunately, his successors and the intellectual elite of the country have downplayed his contribution and denied him the credit that was due to him.

One reason for this could be that the Green Revolution, which changed the face of Indian agriculture, was a complete negation of the Nehruvian consensus that placed the state at the vanguard of economic progress. The principle behind the transformation wrought by the Green Revolution was similar to the template followed by countries in East and Southeast Asia—execution by the private sector, which controlled the means of production, with strong government support and scientific inputs.

Accepting this and giving it the official stamp of approval would have meant having to accept that Nehru's polices had failed and that redemption lay in abandoning it altogether. Had Shastri lived longer, the government might have followed that course of action. But Shastri was succeeded by Nehru's daughter. And the entire intellectual and administrative establishment had, by that time, come to be dominated by an elite that had developed a vested interest in perpetuating the system. Hence, a conspiracy of silence and connivance combined to rob the Indian people of the chance to alter course. The few voices that pointed out the truth and protested were too weak to make a difference and were easily brushed aside.

Agriculture Continues to Falter

Despite the head start provided by the Green Revolution, the farm sector continued to perform poorly under Indira Gandhi. The Fourth Five Year Plan, formulated under her administration, targeted an increase in agricultural production. Even in industry, the planners focused on industries such as fertilisers, agricultural machinery etc., that would support farming activities. Its two main objectives were:

- To provide the conditions necessary for a sustained increase of about 5 percent per annum over the next decade.
- To enable as large a section of the rural population as possible, including the small farmer, the farmer in dry areas and agricultural labourers to participate in development and share its benefits.

However, except for a marked increase in wheat production, the Plan outcomes were again disappointing. Against a targeted food output of 129 million tonnes in 1973–74, the last year of the Plan, actual production was 103 million tonnes. The production of rice, pulses, cotton and jute missed their targets by wide margins.

Two other factors played a major role in this failure. The production of fertilisers touched 3 million tonnes in 1973–74, way short of the targeted figure of 5.5 million tonnes. The targeted increase in the area under irrigation was also missed. Given the tight control that the Indira Gandhi government exercised over every aspect of the Indian economy, the blame for these twin failures must land at her door. Hence, the dream of self-sufficiency in food had to be deferred as India was forced to import 3.6 million tonnes of food grains in 1973 and 4.8 million tonnes in 1974.

India Falls Behind China

India and China started their development journeys at around the same time and, for the first three decades, crawled along neck-and-neck. From 1979, however, China changed trajectory and raced ahead in almost every economic and social sphere. The 1980s, in particular, was when China began to race ahead; so, the Indira Gandhi and Rajiv Gandhi governments that ruled India during that decade will have to bear responsibility for India falling behind.

Like India, China, too, is predominantly an agrarian society. A report by Ashok Gulati and Prerna Terway reveals that, in 2019, China produced farm output worth $1,367 billion, compared to $407 billion for India, despite using a lesser amount of land. This indicates that Chinese productivity on average is three times that of India. The Chinese success in farming has contributed greatly to the eradication of poverty in that country and its entry into the club of upper middle income countries. This upward mobility was enabled mainly by heavy public investment in the farming sector.

Conclusion

In sum, India did attain self-sufficiency in food grains production during the period under review, but the lot of the farmers continued to remain precarious. The failure of the government's education and industrial policies meant that the huge army of unemployed and underemployed rural workers could not upskill themselves and move into the ranks of industrial labour, as was the case in East and Southeast Asia.

By holding back on similar investment and policy support as was provided by the governments of these countries, the governments that ruled India in the first four decades of independence set back the efforts of the Indian farmers to uplift themselves and place the country on a higher trajectory of growth and existence.

6

How Flawed Economic Planning Led to the Nehruvian Rate of Growth

In January 1955, socialism was officially hardwired into the Indian system. At the Congress session in Avadi, Nehru steered through a resolution to "establish a socialist pattern of society where the principal means of production are under social ownership or control."[134] This was followed a year later by the Second Five Year Plan—inspired by the example of the Soviet Union.

Around this time, when the Nehru government was pushing the Second Five Year Plan through Parliament, Reuters came out with an explosive expose in a distant land, reverberations of which ought to have been felt in India but, unfortunately, were not.

According to the newsbreak by John Rettie of Reuters in March 1956, Nikita Khrushchev, the Soviet leader, had delivered a secret Special Report to the twentieth Congress of the Communist Party of the Soviet Union on February 24–25, 1956, in which he denounced his predecessor, the recently deceased Stalin. Though the speech was ostensibly a state secret and meant only for the delegates present at the closed-door session, it was leaked via intermediaries, according to some accounts, by Khrushchev himself. Since it was circulated widely across the world, Nehru and his advisors should have known about the massive human and social cost of Stalin's "success," but they still chose to ignore one of the greatest genocides in the history of mankind.

The following are translated excerpts from the explosive report:

> Stalin acted not through persuasion, explanation and patient cooperation with people, but by imposing his concepts and demanding absolute submission to his opinion. Whoever opposed these concepts or tried to prove his [own] viewpoint, and the correctness of his [own] position was doomed to removal from the leadership collective and to subsequent moral and physical annihilation...
>
> ... It was determined that of the 139 members and candidates of the Central Committee who were elected at the 17th Congress, 98 persons, i.e., 70 per cent, were arrested and shot (mostly in 1937–1938). What was the composition of the delegates to the 17th Congress? ... The only reasons why 70 per cent of the Central Committee members and candidates elected at the 17th Congress were branded as enemies of the Party and of the people were because honest Communists were slandered, accusations against them were fabricated, and revolutionary legality was gravely undermined...
>
> Mass repressions grew tremendously from the end of 1936 after a telegram from Stalin and (Andrey) Zhdanov, dated from Sochi on September 25, 1936, was addressed to (Lazar) Kaganovich, (Vyacheslav) Molotov and other members of the Politbiuro.[135]

So, it was not the Western propaganda that was calling out Stalin's methods; instead, it was being exposed by the Communist Party of Soviet Union itself. It should have served as a warning sign and acted as a speed breaker to Nehru's headlong march towards a socialist pattern of society. But so convinced were the Prime Minister and his advisors about the infallibility of their methods that they chose to ignore the voices that advocated caution.

The Second Five Year Plan failed to deliver on its promise. Planning minister Gulzarilal Nanda warned that the Plan would fall woefully short of the employment target. This alone should have flashed danger signals to the planners and called for a rethinking of the country's economic direction and priorities. But such was the hold of ideology on Nehru, his advisors, and his successors that the Plan document became, arguably, the most important economic document ever drafted in India till Manmohan Singh's 1991 Budget speech that overturned four decades of socialist orthodoxy and set India on the path of economic freedom and progress.

The Plan philosophy, which spread through the sinews of the government and became the economic orthodoxy of the Indian State for decades to come, put into practice the socialist ideas of investment in a large public sector at the expense of the private sector, with emphasis on heavy industry at the expense of consumer goods and a focus on import substitution at the expense of export promotion. This set India on a disastrous course of economic development that cemented its position in the 1960s, 1970s and 1980s as the country with the begging bowl that survived on foreign aid and led inevitably, to near bankruptcy in 1991.

The downslide that began with the Second Plan ate up precious foreign exchange and dried up the supply of scarce foreign funds for other important functions. Despite efforts to spin its success in setting up heavy industries, its gains were doubtful—against the targeted annual growth of 4.5 percent, it achieved 4.27 percent. Its failures on agriculture, employment, and almost every other parameter should have set off alarm bells in the government but such was the strength of the socialist dogma of the Prime Minister that there was no pushback against this.

Conflict over Planning

Soon after Independence, the ideological tussle between Sardar Patel and Nehru came to the fore over economic planning. Though the former was not opposed to the Planning Commission, per se, he wanted it to remain under elected representatives rather than Nehru's favoured model of placing it under a technocrat. Matters came to a head over a draft Congress party resolution that said the Planning Commission would seek to eliminate "the motive of private gain in economic activity." The language closely echoed Nehru's views on the subject, but Patel would have none of it.

But Nehru had the last laugh—once again. Patel died on December 15, 1950. With this, the last fetters on Pandit Nehru's leftwing zeal were removed. He moved quickly to consolidate power in himself. Congress president Purushottamdas Tandon, who had been elected to the post with Patel's backing, resigned in August 1951 and Nehru was elected party president, thus, concentrating the top positions in the government and the party in his own person.

A Flawed "Vision"

When we were in school in the 1970s, our textbooks and teachers would extol Nehru as the Builder of Modern India. This was raised to the level of a dogma and any criticism of his policies was quickly snuffed out. These laudatory references were routinely repeated in high decibel government advertisement campaigns via Indian News Reel short films that were shown in movie halls before every film and full-page advertisements on Republic Day, Independence Day, and Nehru's birthday, which was (and still is) celebrated as Children's Day.

Was he deserving of such adulation? The first Prime Minister undoubtedly has many laudable achievements to his credit—such as the deepening of democracy, the setting up of the IITs, IIMs, Indian Space Research Organisation, the facilities for conducting research on atomic power, among several others. But his biggest failures—in the spheres of economy, administration, and foreign policy—are too glaring not to notice and comment on.

Several experts and analysts have attempted to explain the failure of his economic policies by pointing out that he was following the zeitgeist of his times and that large parts of the world were then in complete thrall of the Soviet Union's Marxist model of economic planning and development. They also point out that there were no alternative systems that could have encouraged him to explore the path that Patel (when he had been alive) and a few economists like B.R. Shenoy were advocating.

But charting new paths and blazing new trails is what truly visionary leaders do. Based on the evidence, it has to be said that Nehru was found wanting on this count. He was just another big name, tall leader who had become a prisoner of his ideology and who refused to consider that there existed alternative paths to national glory.

Alternatives Ignored

There were, in fact, several examples of countries adopting a market-led development model and succeeding. Western Europe had risen from the rubble of the Second World War on the strength of the market. Germany (West Germany) and Austria, which had borne of the brunt of Allied bombings, had risen again. Their success was already being dubbed the Miracle of the Rhine.

Germany's rise from the ashes was led by Chancellor Konrad Adenauer and his Economics Minister Ludwig Erhard, who established an era of rapid economic growth accompanied by low inflation. Experts attribute Germany's post-War economic miracle to Ordoliberal economic policies, which is the German version of liberal economics. The duo cut income taxes sharply and abolished price controls. The removal of price controls, in the face of stiff opposition all round, had a dramatic impact on the economy. It eliminated a burgeoning black market in daily use items including food. With producers now getting remunerative prices, efficiency improved and set the economy on a higher growth path.

Japan's post-War economic revival was powered by government backing for Japanese private businesses, specifically *keiretsus*, which were loosely interconnected business groups that had common interlocking shareholding that came to dominate the Japanese business scene after the

Second World War. By the 1960s, Japan had risen from the atomic bombing of 1945 to emerge as the world's third largest economy after the US and the USSR. Japan's growth was admittedly funded and shepherded by the US, which feared that a poor Japan might find communism attractive and join the Soviet Bloc. But it speaks of the vision of Japan's royal family and its post-War leadership to make peace with the conqueror in order to improve its own position in the comity of nations.

If only Nehru had displayed similar vision and shed his self-defeating Third Worldism, anti-imperialist rhetoric and Soviet-inspired economic worldview, and conjured up the courage to accept that he was leading India down the road of continuing poverty, he might have bundled up the courage to change course. He had unprecedented political and moral authority to do so. There was no leader either in his own party or in the opposition who came close to him in popularity and respect. Yet, he remained a prisoner to his blinkered vision.

US President John F. Kennedy had committed millions of dollars in aid and support to India during and before the 1962 China war. Nehru had not allowed his anti-imperialism to come in the way of seeking and accepting US military aid during and after the India-China war in 1962. According to Bruce Reidel's book *JFK's Forgotten Crisis: Tibet, the CIA, and the Sino-Indian War,* Nehru had requested 250 combat aircraft to help fight the Chinese. In 1963, after the war had ended, the US Air Force, along with the air forces of Britain, Canada, and Australia, carried out air exercises in India as per Nehru's request to send a message that the US was ready to defend India from a future Chinese attack.[136]

A more pragmatic, visionary leader, adept in the art of realpolitik, would have played up the communist threat to extract material and financial benefits from a sympathetic Kennedy administration and led India up the path of growth and development—as post-War Japanese leaders had done, and the then leadership of South Korea and Taiwan were doing. But Nehru had, by this time, become a prisoner to his ideology and preferred the soaring rhetoric of povertarianism, Third Worldism, and Non-Alignment and applause from other Third World leaders and his own coterie of loyal followers to the possibility of bringing about a material uplift in the lot of the countrymen who had elected him.

Indian planners continued to flog the dead horse of socialism even though it had become apparent that it was not delivering the desired results.

The Indian establishment, it seemed, was determined to keep the country poor.

Several Countries Faced the Same Challenges as India

Nehru's backers like repeating ad nauseam how he had to grapple with an impossibly difficult situation—a poor, largely illiterate population, a backward economy, a country devastated by partition, and a weak economy. They claim that the challenges were so great that it would not have been humanly possible for anyone else to have done a better job. What they do not tell you is that several other countries also faced the same situation and managed to overcome the obstacles that stood in their way and forged ahead.

In 1947, India had Asia's only steel plants, its only functional aircraft factory, and large textiles, sugar, and jute industries. A fledgling automobile industry had also begun to take shape in the 1940s and early 1950s, with Hindustan Motors Premier Automobiles, Standard Motors, and Tata Engineering and Locomotive Works leading the way. At that time, Japan's automobile industry was struggling and most of its other industries had been bombed to rubble during the Second World War. No other Asian country had an industrial base comparable to India.

Every country that rose from the ashes of the War—in Western Europe, East Asia and, a few years later, South East Asia—did so by successfully tackling the unique sets of problems and challenges they encountered. They embraced the market, some more cautiously than the others; they welcomed private industry; they emphasised universal education, foreign trade, and strongly repudiated communism. In doing so, they were all going against the conventional wisdom of those times, at least among Third World nations, but that is where their leaders displayed real vision, sagacity, and enterprise.

The results are there for everyone to see.

Around the time that Nehruvian planners were getting busy drawing up the Third Five Year Plan, an East Asian country that had recently been through a brutal war and, like India, had been divided into two, was beginning its journey to First World status.

S Korea's per Capita Income Was 40 Percent Below India's

In the 1950s, South Korea was considered an economic basket case. After the devastating Korean War that left the country partitioned, the country was left with little natural resources, and most of the undivided country's industries were in the North. It was a backward country whose agriculture-based economy was dominated by subsistence farming. In the early 1960s. when Nehru's planners were implementing the Third Five Year Plan, South Korea's per capita income was 40 percent lower than India's. Naturally, domestic savings were abysmally low and a population growth of 3 percent put additional pressure on the already highly dense population of the country. Unemployment was endemic; poverty was all-pervasive; and more than 40 percent of the country's population was suffering from absolute poverty.[137]

Like India, South Korea had embarked upon a policy of import substitution in the immediate aftermath of its partition in 1953. But, unlike India's leaders, the country's authorities realised the futility of this strategy after only six years (1954–60), following a lacklustre performance. So, changing economic course was the obvious solution. But yes, there was a change of government. Prime Minister Chang Myon's Democratic Party ushered in the Second Republic in 1960 that lasted only one year but set South Korea on the path to long-term economic growth. Chang's successor, General Park Chung Hee, who overthrew him in a military coup in 1961, continued his predecessor's anti-communist and pro-business policies and also gave the economy an outward orientation.

In India's case, Nehru's long rule, his stubborn refusal to admit to the failure of his policies and change course, and the elevation of his daughter to the position of Prime Minister within a couple of years of his passing resulted in an inter-generational perpetuation of the same tired and failing system that continued to belie expectations.

In South Korea, the new outward orientation was marked by an export-led strategy. In the 1963–73 period, the rise in exports contributed three times as much to GDP as import substitution did.

These policies enabled South Korea to change from a primarily agricultural economy to an industrial one. The mining and manufacturing sector, which accounted for 12 percent in 1954 had increased its share to 30.2 percent in 1986, while the share of agriculture fell from 44.6 percent to 13.5 percent. The structure of South Korea's foreign trade also changed during this period. In 1962, primary products accounted for 75 percent of exports and industrial products the rest. In 1982, manufactured goods made up 94 percent of exports.[138]

Starting from 40 percent below India, South Korea's per capita income, at more than $33,000 in 2020, was 12 times higher than India's per capita income of about $2,500. In 1990, this figure was nearly $5,000[139], compared to the then Indian per capita income of $375.[140]

The Korean economic miracle, called Miracle of the Han River, was also the result of planning, but, unlike India, its planners were not paralysed by dogma or blindsided by ideology. When their initial policy measures failed to deliver results, as did the import substitution policy, they quickly adopted alternative means.

So, who were the visionaries? Nehru and his daughter, who kept Indians poor, or the South Korean leadership that made their country rich?

Forward thinking leaders with foresight and wisdom always have a Plan B ready. If their Plan A does not deliver the desired results, they quickly make a mid-course correction and bring out Plan B.

Similarly, Taiwan also adopted a market-oriented economic policy that was preceded by aggressive land reforms that removed the landlord class. This resulted in a dramatic upswing in farm yields and rural prosperity and laid the groundwork for the subsequent industrial surge.

A Calamity Averted in Agriculture

In pursuance of his vision of eliminating the profit motive from society and to usher in a socialistic pattern of society in the agricultural sector, Nehru unveiled his most quixotic and potentially most catastrophic economic proposal—collectivisation of agriculture—at the sixty-fourth session of the All India Congress Committee meeting in Nagpur in January 1959.

According to *Encyclopaedia Britannica* this was a

> policy adopted by the Soviet government, pursued most intensively between 1929 and 1933, to transform traditional agriculture in the Soviet Union and to reduce the economic power of the kulaks (prosperous peasants). Under collectivization the peasantry were forced to give up their individual farms and join large collective farms (kolkhozy).[141]

Disaster ensued. "Output fell, but the government, nevertheless, extracted the large amounts of agricultural products it needed to acquire the capital for industrial investment. This caused a major famine in the countryside (1932–33) and the deaths of millions of peasants," according to *Britannica*.

China, too, tried the same experiment, with the same results. *Britannica* noted:

> In 1955 the Maoists speeded up the process of agricultural collectivization. After this came the Great Leap Forward, a refinement of the traditional five-year plans, and other efforts at mobilizing the masses into producing small-scale industries ("backyard steel furnaces") throughout China. The experiment's waste, confusion, and inefficient management combined with natural calamities to produce a prolonged famine (1959–61) that killed 15 to 30 million people.[142]

Nehru was then at the peak of his powers. No one could dare to oppose him or his vision of a socialist utopia, albeit by democratic means. A young Congress leader from Uttar Pradesh alone mustered up the courage to voice the unease in the farming community.

Charan Singh, who later became Prime Minister of India for a few weeks, rose to oppose Nehru's proposal. He strongly opposed the Prime Minister's dangerous dogma.

Singh's bold and brave intervention, thus, saved not only Indian farmers but also the larger rural community from the threat of widespread disruption and mass-scale misery that collectivisation could have led to. This has been discussed in detail in Chapter 5.

Temples of Modern India Fail to Deliver Desired Results

At school, we were taught that Nehru's Five Year Plans, his strategy of building big dams and establishing heavy industries, encapsulated in his Temples of Modern India strategy, and his focus on socialism and import substitution had laid the foundation for the development of India. His family's patronage system had, by then, captured nearly every institution of the State. The left wing intellectuals—who controlled the media, academia, and the public discourse—were beholden to the government of the day. So, there was no pushback against this narrative, and everyone believed it to be the truth.

But this begs the question: if the Nehruvian model of development was, indeed, such a good thing, why was India still so poor? Why was the country home to the largest number of illiterate people in the world? Why was unemployment rampant? Why were there shortages of almost every item—from food to cars and scooters, to cement, steel, gas and telephone connections, and newsprint?

Back then, there were no 24×7 private news channels. The state-owned Doordarshan and All India Radio disseminated only what the government wanted the people to hear. Low literacy levels ensured that few people read newspapers, which were anyway mostly controlled by people affiliated to the establishment. And very few people travelled abroad. So, there was little awareness about how far India was falling behind not only the European nations but also its peers in Asia.

Meanwhile, there was high decibel propaganda about India being the global leader of the Third World and the Non-Aligned Movement and how Nehru and Indira Gandhi had enhanced India's self-respect across the world by standing up to the imperialistic West. This served to create an alternative reality far removed from the truth that diverted attention of the people from their grim everyday struggles.

My father, who was reasonably well-travelled, and otherwise a diehard Nehru fan, used to derisively call this claim of being the leader of the developing world as "*Andho mein kana raja*." (In the land of the blind, the one-eyed is king).

This carefully curated fiction began to unravel post-1991, when a financial crisis was followed by the opening up of the country's economy. The resulting information explosion and rising of foreign travel by Indians made it starkly apparent that stories about the successes of Nehruvian socialism had been vastly exaggerated.

Far from being modern, the India that Nehru and his successors had built was, in fact, broken and standing on very shaky foundations. The rot, as we have seen in previous chapters, began to set in when the death of Sardar Patel removed the last political check on Nehru's socialist zeal.

Plans Found Wanting in Welfare and Delivery of Public Goods

The Socialist Bloc lost steam and ran into quicksand in the late 1980s and early 1990s—around the same time that the Nehruvian model finally bankrupted India. But all the countries of the Eastern Bloc had at least guaranteed 100 percent literacy and education, housing, clothing, healthcare, clean water and air, not to mention a minimum standard of living for all the people living within their territories.

Nehru's much-vaunted ideal of a socialistic pattern of society had failed miserably to even ensure that. On social welfare, too, Nehruvian planning was found wanting. Although the provision of public goods received a lot of rhetorical attention from Nehru, Indira Gandhi, Rajiv

Gandhi, and their ministers, actual allocations were much lower than for the government's economic goals.

In his seminal work *India Is Broken*, Ashoka Mody noted: "Public policy did not work for the general welfare during the socialist years or later. Modern India's propellant force then and ever since has been its deeply unequal development process."

This has been hanging around India's neck like an albatross. It is well known that, since the Industrial Revolution two hundred and fifty years ago, no society has been able to achieve manufacturing excellence and mass prosperity without first making provisions for spreading education, especially among women, near universal healthcare, and dignified urban living conditions. By neglecting these especially in the first four decades of Independence, India's rulers have hamstrung the country's development potential and made it that much more difficult for succeeding governments to cover the huge backlog and catch up with our peers.

Unemployment Keeps Rising

The unemployment plaguing the economy reached crisis proportions by the late 1960s. Frustrated youth gave vent to their anger by joining the Naxalite movement in urban West Bengal. Although this was ruthlessly crushed, the underlying reasons remained unaddressed.

India's biggest challenge, Nehru had declared on October 2, 1950, Mahatma Gandhi's birth anniversary, was the removal of poverty and unemployment from the country. But, in an unfortunate pattern that would repeat itself over and over again throughout his long rule and that of his daughter, there was a wide chasm between rhetoric and action.

A 1954 National Statistical Survey estimated that about 1 percent of Indians were openly unemployed, i.e. they did not have a job. But this did not paint the full picture. A large number of people were underemployed. Most such people were in the farming sector and would sit idle between seasons. In urban and semi-urban settings, especially in the unorganised sector, families would spread the available work among its members. This was estimated at 15 percent. In sum, the actual unemployment rate was estimated at 16 percent (1 percent + 15 percent).[143] Given India's effective labour force of 167.5 million then, the number of unemployed were estimated at 26 million. In 1958, P.C. Mahalanobis estimated the unemployment in 1955 to be at 25 million.

What was needed was rapid, labour-intensive industrialisation to absorb this massive, mostly illiterate mass of humanity into productive employment and simultaneous investment in primary education to prepare India's largely rural farmhands for work on the factory floor. Instead, the Nehru government launched its misconceived Temples of Modern India policy of investing in capital-intensive heavy industries that would, if successful, generate mass employment after a generation. So, even in the best-case scenario, India's hungry, poor and illiterate population of millions was being asked to wait a full generation before they could even hope to see light at the end of the tunnel. This elitist act of exclusion ensured that, in reality, many people were still waiting for their long night of despair to end in 1991, when the Nehruvian economic mantra was finally abandoned. This misguided focus on heavy industry also meant that India lost the most important opportunity of carving a niche for itself in the world market for low-end labour-intensive products that could have generated employment for its millions-strong army of unemployed and underemployed people.

But the inability of his government to generate employment did nothing to blunt Nehru's soaring rhetoric. Summoning his mastery over words, he acknowledged the unemployment crisis plaguing the economy; he lamented that Indian universities were churning out graduates and post-graduates but imparting little knowledge. Finding employment for such people, he said, was proving difficult. Just as he blamed Indian farmers for poor harvests, absolving his government of all responsibility, here, he was shifting the blame to the universities and the candidates for their failure to find employment. Despite the lack of any cogent plan to increase employment, Nehru declared, rather grandly, at the Avadi Congress party session in January 1955, that his government would eradicate unemployment over the next 10 years, in pursuit of a socialistic pattern of society.

Meanwhile, India's loss was Taiwan's and South Korea's gain. The space vacated by Japan at the low end of the market was filled by products manufactured in these countries. Nehru's short-sightedness and lack of vision, thus, gave them a free pass into the global value chain. By the mid-1960s, South Korea was beginning to make a name for itself as an exporter of clothes, cotton textiles and footwear and had also begun exporting small volumes of small motors, transformers, and radios, while India's export basket had barely changed since Independence and still comprised basic commodities such as tea, jute, cotton yarn, and cotton textiles. A few Indian companies had begun exporting light engineering products, but their volume was very small.

The draft outline of the Fourth Five Year Plan gave vent to the frustration in official circles over the economy's inability to generate sufficient employment for the country's burgeoning population. "Successive Plans on development are unable to find gainful employment for the net addition to the labour force and continue to add to the backlog of unemployed persons," it said of the previous three Plans. Surveys showed that the number of unemployed had risen from about 25 million in 1955 to between 30 million and 35 million a decade later.[144] That means, far from solving the employment problem, Nehruvian planning had been adding between half a million to a million per year to the number of unemployed youth in the country.

Nehru's Reign Leaves 60 Percent Indians in Severe Poverty; India Falls Behind China, Other Asian Peers Under Indira

Between 1980 and 1984, more or less coinciding with Indira Gandhi's second stint as Prime Minister, India began to fall behind in the race with a new bunch of Asian competitors. Thailand, Indonesia, the Philippines and Malaysia began to produce low-end labour-intensive products and began to clock annual growth rates of 6 percent to 8 percent or double that of India. With Indian companies unable to compete in the international market, and not allowed to grow domestically, employment generation became the obvious casualty.

By this time, it was glaringly apparent that Nehruvian policies and socialist controls were holding the economy back but Indira Gandhi made only a very feeble effort to remove the chains that held Indian industry back. The result was a slight improvement in growth rates but this was not enough to solve the massive unemployment crisis that had reached gargantuan proportions since the beginning of planning during her father's reign.

In the mid-1980s, the total number of unemployed in India was estimated at 40–45 million from 30–35 million at the end of Nehru's term.[145] That means in the two decades since his demise—during which his daughter was Prime Minister for 16 years—the unemployment rate rose at more or less the same rate as it did in the last 10 years of his rule.

So, all the socialist rhetoric about eradicating unemployment and providing succour to the poor was just that—rhetoric with no substance. After 17 years of being ruled by Nehru and 16 years by Indira Gandhi, Indians were not too much better off than they had been in 1947. Ashoka Mody observed:

> ...progress in the Nehru years barely touched large parts of the country, particularly those in the rural areas... Through the Nehru era, 60 percent or more of the Indian population remained in severe poverty. For this large fraction of Indians, the country made virtually no progress.[146]

By 1977, when a non-Congress government came to power at the Centre for the first time, "India had been ruled for nearly all of its years an independent nation by Jawaharlal Nehru and Indira Gandhi and the failures of their rule were abundantly available."[147]

Indians were not more literate, more well-to-do, or more employed. The government had also failed to build sufficient numbers of village roads, rural health services, sanitation, schools, and infrastructure.

First Five Year Plan Puts India on the Growth Trajectory

The First Five Year Plan (1951–56) prioritised mass education, agricultural productivity, inflation control and rehabilitation of refugees, and was based on the Harrod–Domar Model, with a few modifications. It was a propitious beginning. The Plan implementation was successful. The GDP growth during the Plan period averaged 3.6 percent per annum against the targeted growth of 2.1 percent. Good monsoons ensured high farm yields, and this boosted both per capita incomes as well as foreign exchange reserves.

Several large dams, which were central to the Second Five Year Plan, such as Bhakra Nangal, Damodar Valley and Hirakud, were initiated during this period, as were the Indian Institutes of Technology.

Second Five Year Plan Begins the Downslide

The success of the First Plan is believed to have lulled the planners into a sense of complacency—that they had placed agriculture on the path of self-sustaining growth and that primary education did not need the kind of laser focus it had received in the 1951–56 period.

By this time, Nehru was completely in thrall of P.C. Mahalanobis's model that prioritised heavy industries, the public sector, and import substitution. During the Second Plan period, in addition to the hydroelectric power projects initiated during the closing stages of the First Plan, new steel plants were set up at Bhilai (with Soviet help), Durgapur (UK), and Rourkela (Germany).

The highly capital-intensive Plan led to a shortage of precious foreign exchange and insufficient funding for consumer goods. Given the government's goal of establishing a socialist pattern of society, it tightened licensing requirements for industry, and this led to shortages of items of everyday use, the emergence of an organised black market and inflation, even as rapid population growth slowed down per capita income growth to minuscule levels. Employment generation, too, fell well short of target. This was a structural problem—a capital-intensive Plan could not simultaneously be labour-intensive. Therefore, it was unsuitable for the economic environment that existed then. Overall, the GDP grew at 4.27 percent per annum during this period, compared to the targeted rate of 4.5 percent.

Third Five Year Plan Falls Woefully Short

The failure of the Second Plan did not deter Nehru and his advisors. Far from being chastised by the failure of their grandiose ideas, they doubled down on taking India further down the path they had set out on in the Third Five Year Plan (1961–66). The 1962 War with China came as a rude shock and exposed the unpreparedness of the Indian economy to absorb any shocks. Inflation soared. Another war, this time with Pakistan, in 1965 and a grievous drought in 1964–65 dealt severe blows to the already weak Indian economy.

Nehru passed away in 1964, and his successor, Lal Bahadur Shastri, initiated a major agricultural reforms programme, which culminated in the Green Revolution that made India self-sufficient in food grains for the first time in decades.

Nehru's stubborn refusal to encourage foreign trade and the reluctance of his daughter, who succeeded Shastri as Prime Minister after a gap of two years, to change course hit home hard in 1966, when a balance of payments crisis confronted the government. The country was facing a huge trade deficit; it was dependent on foreign aid; exports were negligible; and foreign investments were actively discouraged. The government of Indira Gandhi, thus, had no option but to approach the International Monetary Fund (IMF) for a loan. The rupee was devalued for the first time after Independence on June 6, 1966.

There was a massive fall in food grains production—from 82 million tonnes to 72 million tonnes—during the Third Plan. India also continued to fall well short of meeting its employment targets, thus, adding to the growing backlog of unemployed or underemployed people. Given the multiplicity of failures on several fronts, it was not surprising that GDP growth averaged a miserable 2.4 percent against the target of 5.5 percent.

Plan Holidays for Three Years

The massive failure of the Third Five Year Plan forced the government to defer the fourth plan and declare three back-to-back annual plans to set the economy back on an even keel. The government used this interregnum between the Third and Fourth Plans to close the economic gaps created by the failure of the Third Plan. These helped India get back on the growth path, which, however, was still way below the double-digit figures clocked by the Asian Tigers.

Fourth Plan Also Falls Short of Targets

The Fourth Plan (1969–74) set out to correct the concentration of wealth in the hands of a tiny business and political elite. This had begun to become apparent as a result of socialism and licensing, which resulted in rampant crony capitalism and black marketing. This Plan, too, continued to hurtle down the doomed path of self-reliance and import substitution and was ostensibly focused on growth with stability.

This was the peak of Indira Gandhi's socialist avatar. She nationalised fourteen major commercial banks, gave the emotionally appealing but ultimately empty call of *Garibi Hatao* in the run-up to the Lok Sabha elections of 1971, and raised income tax rates to 97.5 percent.

Naturally, tax evasion soared, and corruption became all-pervasive. However, food grain production soared as a result of the Green Revolution, and India headed rapidly towards self-sufficiency in food grains.

The Plan failed to meet most of its growth targets, as India grew at 3.3 percent, against the targeted rate of 5.6 percent.

Fifth Five Year Plan: India Grows But Slowly

This Plan (1974–78) continued the government's focus on *Garibi Hatao*, despite very limited success in alleviating poverty. On employment generation, too, the government had fallen woefully behind its targets after the failure of three previous Plans. The Plan, however, saw the GDP growth, at 4.8 percent, outpace the very modest target of 4.4 percent.

Rolling Plans (1978–80)

The Morarji Desai government that came to power in 1977, rejected the fifth Plan that had been drawn up by the previous Indira Gandhi government and replaced it with a Sixth Plan. However, Indira Gandhi returned to power in 1980 and scrapped this plan and replaced it her own Sixth Plan.

Sixth Five Year Plan

Indira Gandhi's spell in the political wilderness seemed to have taught her that the Indian electorate could no longer be persuaded to support her solely on the strength of emotional but vacuous socialist rhetoric.

In the Sixth Five Year Plan (1980–85), she took baby steps towards dismantling the socialist edifice that her father and her previous administration had spent more than three decades putting in place. Many price controls were eased or abolished and industry, though still in fetters, was given relatively greater freedom to operate than before. This small step had a very positive impact on the economy. GDP growth during the Plan period jumped to 5.7 percent per annum, compared to the target of 5.2 percent. This was the best India had ever done over a five-year period.

But this was still only a fraction of the steroid-charged growth rates that the Asian Tigers and the newly liberalising ASEAN countries managed. India remained a poor country even as South Korea, which began its development journey almost one-and-a-half decades after India, rose to middle-income status during this decade.

Seventh Five Year Plan

For the first time since the end of the First Plan, the government was not playing catch-up with the missed targets of the previous Plan period. The farm sector had done well in the previous Plan period; inflation had been reined in; and the balance of payments situation did not look threatening, though employment figures still lagged behind the target.

The Seventh Five Year Plan (1985–90) stressed the adoption of newer technologies, better productivity, agricultural development, full provision of *roti*, *kapda* and *makaan for* everyone, social justice, and strengthening of the economy.

The economy grew at 6.01 percent, compared to the target growth rate of 5 percent.

Nehruvianism Continues to Haunt the Indian Economy

Jawaharlal Nehru passed away in 1964, but his flawed economic legacy and self-defeating faith in socialism and in an all-pervasive and heavy-handed government continued to inform and dominate the thinking of his successors, especially his daughter, and much of India's officialdom. But, by 1991, more than four decades of Nehruvian economic policies had fundamentally weakened the Indian economy. Imports had risen over the years, especially during the Seventh Plan period, and the decades-long neglect of exports meant the country was not generating enough foreign exchange to pay for its needs. Rupee trade with the Soviet Bloc had ensured that India did not need hard currencies to pay for a large part of its imports.

However, the collapse of the socialist bloc and the start of the Gulf War brought things to a head and created conditions for the perfect economic storm. With Iraq and Kuwait, two of India's main crude oil suppliers, caught at the centre of the war, the external situation took a turn for the worse. Crude prices surged, and this made the already poor balance of payments situation worse. With the rupee value in free fall, India's foreign exchange reserves fell to a precarious level—just enough to pay for three weeks of imports.

The government, which was on the brink of defaulting on its international financial obligations, was unable to pass the annual Budget in February 1991, after Moody's downgraded India's bond ratings. The IMF and the World Bank suspended their loan and assistance programmes.

This combination of factors made it frightfully expensive and almost impossible for India to borrow money from the international markets. The government was forced to mortgage part of its gold reserves with the Bank of England to raise money to stave off an international bankruptcy.

This was much worse and more humiliating than going around the world with the proverbial begging bowl, but it was almost inevitable. The road that Nehru and his elite band of leftist followers had embarked upon in the mid-1950s had led predictably to this economic *cul-de-sac.*

India had only one option—abandon the shibboleths and the holy cows of the past, and then reform, liberalise, globalise, and embrace the markets.

Where Planning Failed

When the Nehruvian economic model was finally given a burial in 1991, very few people shed tears for it, except a few

Congressmen, some bureaucrats and a host of big businessmen who were its main beneficiaries.

Planning and the socialist model kept India poor and sealed its image as the country with a begging bowl. As a student, it used to make my blood boil when I read the very occasional but usually pejorative mention of India and Indians in the foreign press. In the 1980s, four decades after Independence, India was still largely illiterate, mostly poor, full of slums, and ridden with corruption. Urban infrastructure was in a shambles. Rural infrastructure was practically non-existent. Large sections of the population did not have access to safe drinking water. And unemployment was all pervasive.

Nehruvian planning had failed to deliver on almost every count. That is because Indian planners often had their heads in the clouds. Projects were invariably delayed—because of poor plan architecture, inefficiency and corruption. This inevitably led to cost overruns and delayed the downstream benefits that were supposed to accrue.

Retired senior bureaucrat S.S. Gill mentioned in his book, *The Dynasty*, how political pressure led to distortions in the planning process and ensured that Plan targets were seldom achieved. "States seldom exerted to raise adequate resources or to enforce even mildly radical measures,"[148] he wrote.

The government's failures in the fields of education, unemployment, public goods, etc. have been discussed in other chapters in this book.

Marxist Aristocracy and the Nehruvian Rate of Growth

Who was responsible for the miserable state of affairs of an overwhelming majority of Indians? Nehru himself accepted the failure of planning. "One thing that distresses me very greatly is that... there is a good number of people who have not profited by planning and whose poverty is abysmal and most painful,"[149] Nehru told the Lok Sabha on December 11, 1963, in a surprising display of candour.

The political and intellectual establishment was aware of these failures. The abysmally slow rate of growth could be laid squarely at the doors of Jawaharlal Nehru and his daughter Indira Gandhi, who had ruled India for a combined 33 years. It was their embrace of socialism, licensing, disdain for the private sector and rejection of foreign trade that had kept India poor and precluded it from achieving its economic potential.

But no aristocracy has ever accepted blame for the misery of its subjects. So, Marxist intellectuals who controlled the levers of public discourse took it upon themselves to divert attention from Nehru and his daughter and decided to blame the first Prime Minister's object of dislike—the Hindu civilisation—for the failures of Nehruvian economic policies and the anemic growth of 3.5–4 percent since Independence. Delhi School of Economics professor Raj Krishna coined the term "Hindu rate of growth"[150] in 1978. It was interpreted pejoratively to mean the alleged Hindu outlook of fatalism and lack of interest in material benefits, which, according to India's then leftwing establishment, was responsible for India's economic backwardness.

The authors of India's continued economic stagnation were shifting blame for their own failures to a group of people who had been kept in ideological chains and denied true economic freedom for three decades and more. The term soon gained great currency in not only India but also other parts of the world.

It seemed as if India's intellectual class was shaking off all responsibility for the destitution that they had inflicted upon their fellow countrymen even as they took it upon themselves to censor any negative views on Nehru.

Did Nehru Consider Indians Lazy?

Did Nehru lack confidence in the ability of Indians? And did his condescension towards India colour his style of governance that left so many millions of people without even the most basic means of sustenance? He has himself admitted to having a Euro-centric worldview and accepted that he looked at India not as an Indian but through European eyes. "I am the last Englishman to rule India," he confided to US Ambassador John Kenneth Galbraith.[151]

Years earlier, in his court trial of 1922, Nehru had said:

> Less than ten years ago, I returned from England after a long stay there.... I looked upon the world almost from an Englishman's standpoint... as much prejudiced in favour of England and the English as it was possible for an Englishman to be.

Refuting Prime Minister Modi's charge that Nehru had called Indians lazy, his great-granddaughter Priyanka Gandhi Vadra released a copy of the speech the PM had quoted. According to this version, the first Prime Minister of India, said:

> Our people, forgetting to trust themselves, think that other people will help them. Our village people are strong

> and nice. It has become a habit that instead of taking matters in their own hands they lean on officers and the government... Communities don't progress with the help of officers, they progress on their own strength.
>
> The only yardstick to measure progress is how 40 crore people of India move forward. The community grows through its hard work... Look at the countries that are happy and prosperous. How did they become prosperous? Through hard work. Be it European nations or American or Asian countries that are prosperous, it is hard work and unity that is behind their prosperity. Without these attributes progress cannot be made... In our India, generally the habit of working very hard has not been developed. It is not our fault, habits are formed due to circumstances.
>
> But the thing is that we do not work as hard as Europeans, Japanese, Chinese, Russians or Americans. Don't think that they became prosperous through magic, but they became prosperous through hard work and intelligence... We can also move forward with hardwork and intelligence. There is no other way.[152]

A plain reading of this speech shows that there is merit in the charge that India's first Prime Minister thought Indians were less hardworking than the citizens of other countries and were, therefore, hardwired to be less successful than Europeans, Japanese, Chinese, Russians or Americans. The comments also suggest a contempt for his countrymen that can only perhaps be explained by his Eurocentric mental make-up.

Why Nehruvian Planning Failed

As a result of the policies followed by governments between 1947 and the start of the liberalisation process, India's share of world trade fell from 2.4 percent in 1947 to 0.4 percent in

1990[153], thus, depriving two generations of Indians an avenue to a better life. Nehruvian planning failed because it was a top-down model rather than a bottom-up one. He also lacked the managerial skills, the patience and the money to implement his grandiose plans. The bureaucracy began to grow and spread its tentacles into every sphere of society and business, which it was not trained to manage, and, soon, inefficiency, sloth and corruption began to rear their ugly heads.

A country marches ahead on the strength of its systems. In the post-World War II world, several dozen countries gained independence from their colonial masters. The choice before them was clear: they could opt for a free market economy; or they could choose to follow the Soviet Union's socialist model of development, where the state would own all, or almost all, the means of production.

Taken in by communist propaganda, lured by the apparent success of the Soviet model and led, in many cases, by Marxist leaders, many countries chose the latter. India debated the issue animatedly, its leaders loudly disagreeing with each other on the direction the economy of the newly independent nation should adopt.

Then, following the death of Sardar Patel in 1950, Nehru bulldozed his socialist ideas through the party and the government, and used the strength of his personal charisma and soaring rhetoric to divert attention from its failures.

Indians had never experienced fast growth and had no idea what they were missing out on. So, they accepted the Nehruvian rate of growth as the default. And therein lay the tragedy of the Nehruvian dream.

7

Corruption, Crony Capitalism Rule the Roost

In 1974, my uncle (*meshomoshai*), my mother's eldest sister's husband, decided to add a first floor to his beautiful single-storied bungalow in Calcutta. A doctor who had retired from government service a few years previously, he was, like many people of his generation, a strict Gandhian—austere and simple in his personal habits despite his successful post-retirement private practice—and a fanatical supporter of Jawaharlal Nehru, Indira Gandhi, and the Congress party.

This innocuous decision—of extending his house—brought him into conflict with the government he had served and the party he had supported all his life. The law, as it existed then, mandated a license to buy construction goods like cement and steel. Strict socialist controls had created chronic shortages in these critical items and given birth to an "official" black market in which licenses were being openly bought and sold. Government officials in charge of issuing licenses demanded bribes in return for issuing permits. Depending on the location, there were unofficial rate cards for permits for various quantities of these materials.

Readers born in post-liberalisation India will find it difficult to imagine such a dystopian past, but this was a reality and a fact of daily life in the socialist India of Nehru and Indira Gandhi. If you did not grease the right palms, you would not be able to buy not only steel or cement but also scooters and cars; if you did not know a senior official or an MLA or MP, you could not get a gas or telephone connection; and if you did not pay the visiting petty official his *salami*, you could receive a cease and desist notice that would stall work on your under construction house.

My uncle, being a principled Gandhian, would have none of this. He refused to pay speed money and would diligently visit the relevant office to follow up with the officials concerned to issue the permits he required to buy steel and cement. After more than six months, he began to feel frustrated at the lack of progress. But even then, he refused to blame his favourite political leaders who had put in place the system that was harassing him. Instead, he blamed the corruption and inefficiency of petty local officials for giving Nehru and Indira Gandhi a bad name. He refused to consider the possibility of the bribes making their way all the way to the top of the political and administrative food chain.

Finally, my aunt took matters into her hand. My second aunt, her younger sister, was married to a powerful minister in the Siddhartha Shankar Ray ministry. She sought his help. And, lo and behold, the precious permits were delivered within a short while. My Gandhian uncle was furious when he found out, but pragmatism won the day. He was happy that he did not have to pay a bribe.

Restrictive Rules Forced Everyone to Pay Bribes

It was not just businessmen and politicians who were indulging in corruption. Such was the stranglehold of a completely unnecessary plethora of rules and regulations that even the common man had no option but to pay bribes and speed money to access simple, everyday amenities, goods, and services.

Honesty and transparency breed trust between people and between rulers and the ruled. The opposite is also true. The multiplicity of restrictive rules and regulations that encompassed all facets of economic life in India had created fertile grounds for corruption to thrive. Ruling party politicians had become very adept at using their discretionary powers to dispense favours by bypassing norms in lieu of benefits for themselves.

According to a 1998 IMF working paper titled "Corruption Around the World: Causes, Consequences, Scope, and Cures" by Vito Tanzi,

> the causes or factors that promote corruption are those that affect demand (by the public) for corrupt acts and those that affect the supply (by public officials) of acts of corruption. Among the factors affecting demand for corruption, the most important are (1) regulations and authorizations; (2) certain characteristics of the tax system; (3) certain spending decisions; (4) Provision of goods and services at below market prices. Among the factors affecting the supply of acts of corruption are (1) the bureaucratic tradition; (2) the level of public sector wages; (3) the penalty systems; (4) institutional controls; (5) the transparency of rules, laws, and processes; and (6) the examples set by the leadership.[154]

These were just as relevant in earlier eras as well. If one considers these ten factors, one will notice that the Nehruvian state falls short on each of these criteria, and these encourage the breaking of rules and provide not only a fillip to but an incentive for corruption. Each of these set the ground for abuse of public office for private gain. This is not to say that corruption does not exist in the private sector. It does and is every bit as pernicious as official corruption, but it does not strictly fall under the rubric of this book.

Corruption Breeds Inefficiencies

In *India Is Broken*, Ashoka Mody pointed out how, in societies in which many people are corrupt, the likelihood of being caught and punished for corruption is limited because those mandated to catch and prosecute the dishonest are themselves crooked. When more and more people take to unethical means, the productivity of the society suffers and gives birth to a "bad equilibrium."

Within a few years of Independence, without Gandhi to maintain the moral compass of the party in place, the Congress became an organisation of opportunistic politicians eager to

> grab the spoils of office, which were becoming ever more plentiful as India expanded its anti-poverty and development spending. The party's leaders and members amassed fortunes by bestowing jobs (in relief works, education, and other services), lucrative contracts (for village wells, roads, and other infrastructure), and discounted loans.[155]

The *Time* magazine summed it up succinctly in 1951 by declaring the Congress as a "sprawling conglomerate" that lacked "a unifying purpose" following Independence, many of whose leaders were "time serving officeholders" who were "black marketeers."[156] It cannot be that Nehru was unaware of these undeserving leaders and their kleptocratic tendencies but he chose to ignore them for the sake of political expediency. His famous pre-Independence declaration that "in free India, [the] corrupt and [the] black marketeers will be hanged from the nearest lamp post,"[157] it turned out, was merely soaring rhetoric and not a declaration of intent.

Soon, government officials began to demand kickbacks to award contracts, jobs and licenses for producing and importing goods. This meant a siphoning of a portion of the already limited development budget of the country, leaving mere crumbs for the benefit of the common man.

Swedish Nobel laureate economist Gunnar Myrdal, who tried to draw up a blueprint for India's development but gave up in despair, was scathing in his assessment of India's development journey in the first two decades after Independence. In 1968, he said that all the gains had accrued to industrialists, big merchants, and other privileged classes, even as relentless price rise had eaten away at the purchasing power of the masses.[158]

The stringent licensing and tax regime in the country provided a perverse incentive for people to pay bribes for even normal, everyday transactions. As seen in the example of my uncle, even common people were forced to pay bribes for mundane activities like buying materials essential for building or repairing houses.

The stakes were higher for businesses. Their businesses could come to a standstill if they refused to pay up. Not only did they have to pay money to ensure the continuation of their businesses, many of them also employed large teams of lobbyists and brokers to ensure that their rivals were denied licenses and permits. This effectively kept competition at bay, created an economy of shortages, and paved the way for black marketing to thrive, creating more avenues for corruption, bribes and illegal aggrandisement.

Nehru Ignores Jeep Scandal

The first major corruption scandal to hit India after Independence was the Jeep Scandal, in which Krishna Menon, as High Commissioner to the UK, ignored protocols and placed a Rs 80 lakh order for 2,000 refurbished Jeeps for the Indian Army at the price of brand new ones. The vendor was an obscure company that was given a hefty advance, but it delivered only 155 Jeeps, none of which were accepted by the Ministry of Defence. No one was found guilty in the investigations that followed. This set a bad example. Krishna Menon was rehabilitated and appointed India's Defence Minister after a few years.

Then, in the 1950s, businessman Haridas Mundhra, who had funded the party, got the government-controlled LIC to buy his company's shares at inflated prices. This cost the then Finance Minister T.T. Krishnamachari his job when the truth came out. There were whispers that he had been made a fall guy to save higher ups.[159]

This, too, set another bad example and provided a fillip to the growing cult of corruption in the Indian government. Instead of taking steps to crack down on the rising tide of corruption afflicting his government and the country as a direct consequence of his highly restrictive policies, Nehru dismissed concerns over the issue as overblown and exaggerated. He wrote to Jagjivan Ram, "People in high office tend to attract wild allegations." According to him, the real problem was not corruption, per se, but the tendency of people to complain too much about corruption. This, he said quite disingenuously, "creates an atmosphere of corruption. People feel they live in a climate of corruption, and they get corrupted themselves."[160]

It is his inaction in cases of corruption and statements like these that brushed the issue of corruption under the carpet that allowed the cancer of corruption to spread across every sinew of the government and society.

Santhanam Committee Report Exposes Can of Worms

When I was in school in the 1970s and early 1980s, we were taught that the Nehru era was some kind of an idyll—an idealistic period of national reconstruction when honesty marked India's public life. The few rare and sporadic instances of corruption were immediately nipped in the bud by the Prime Minister who presided over a sort of socialist *Satya Yug*. Recent political developments have also created an impression in large sections of civil society that evils like crony capitalism have only recently raised their ugly heads in India.

Nothing could be further from the truth. By 1962, fifteen years after Independence, governance in India, both at the Centre and in the states, was riddled with corruption and this was causing disquiet among those of Mahatma Gandhi's disciples who still retained the idealism, austere habits, and high principles that had informed his leadership of the freedom movement.

In June 1962, during a debate in Parliament on the Home Ministry's demands, several MPs expressed serious concern about the growing menace of corruption in the government. In response, then Home Minister Lal Bahadur Shastri formed a committee headed by Congress member K. Santhanam and comprising five other MPs and two officials to "review the problem of corruption and make suggestions" to deal with it.[161]

Prime Minister Nehru was still in the saddle and was the unquestioned leader of the Congress party and the government, and so, the committee obviously could not have been constituted without his concurrence and blessings.

The report, which was submitted in 1964, was a scathing indictment of Nehru's reign. In a severe condemnation of the leadership displayed by the Prime Minister and his handpicked team of administrators, it said:

> Complaints against the highly placed in public life were not dealt with in the manner that they should have been dealt with if public confidence had to be maintained. Weakness in this respect created cynicism and the growth of the belief that while Governments were against corruption they were not against corrupt individuals, if such individuals had the requisite amount of power, influence and protection.[162]

It went on to say:

> ...In the emerging Indian society with its emphasis on purposively initiated process of urbanisation, alongside of

> the weakening of the social mores of the simpler society, signs are visible of materialism, growing impersonalism, importance of status resulting from possession of money and economic power, group loyalties, intensification of parochial affinities, unwillingness or inability to deal with deviations from the highest standards of political, economic and social ethics, profession of faith in the rule of law and disregard thereof where adherence thereto is not convenient.[163]

It did not end there and went on to elaborate:

> The rapid expansion of Governmental activities in new fields involving expenditure of the order of 1,000 crores of rupees a year afforded to the unscrupulous elements in the public service and public life unprecedented opportunities for acquiring wealth by dubious methods. To this must be added the unfortunate decline of the real incomes of various sections of the community, and particularly that a large part of which is found in Government employment.[164]

Thus, this was not only a chargesheet against the government's lackadaisical approach to curbing corruption but also its management of the economy.

Almost anticipating Rajiv Gandhi's lament on power brokers taking over the system two decades later, the report states:

> Where there is power and discretion, there is always the possibility of abuse, more so when the power and discretion have to be exercised in the context of scarcity and controls and pressure to spend public money. The absence of a machinery for appeals other than inside the hierarchy and of a machinery for redress of grievances contributed to the growth of an impression of arbitrariness

on the part of the executive. Consequently, there has been a phenomenal increase in the number of peddlers of influence.[165]

How Crony Capitalism Worked

The Second Five Year Plan had, as we have seen, led to a severe foreign exchange shortage. Economist I.G. Patel, who helped draw the Plan document, later admitted that the severe foreign exchange controls imposed in 1956–57 were not inspired by "socialism." Rather, they were a panic reaction to the sudden and unforeseen drainage of foreign exchange. "No one consciously initiated the policy," he said, adding that the severe restrictions and stringent licensing of imports "was based on no theory or philosophy" because "everyone was surprised by the severity of the exchange crisis that hit us."[166]

Once imposed, however, import controls took on a life of their own. The government was forced to clamp down on new firms and the expansion plans of existing ones in order to conserve scarce foreign exchange. As a result, business houses with production licenses now needed import licenses for the import of capital goods and so, needed to approach the "capital goods committee." The Second Plan had set targets for production of various items that were not fixed. These targets were cited or raised, depending on which business house had applied for a license and which industrialist had won the government's favour. The import targets and foreign exchange allocations, thus, came to depend on the capricious whims of the ruling party politicians and senior bureaucrats who had the wherewithal to reach out to them.[167]

"It is well known that large industrial houses maintain liaison officers in Delhi for business and social contacts with senior persons in the Government and seek to influence the exercise of discretionary power in their favour," an official enquiry into licensing practices noted.[168]

That is about as direct and damaging a charge against Nehru's governance standards as anything his later opponents have accused him of. Without giving it the name, the enquiry report calls out the early contours of crony capitalism.

The Santhanam Committee noted a few years later:

> "Speed money" is reported to have become a fairly common type of corrupt practice particularly in matters relating to grant of licences, permits, etc... It was stated by a Secretary that even after the order had been passed the fact of the passing of such order is communicated to the person concerned, and the order itself is kept back till the unfortunate applicant has paid appropriate gratification to the subordinate concerned. Besides being a most objectionable corrupt practice, this custom of speed money has become one of the most serious causes of delay and inefficiency. For some reason, the report did not mention institutional corruption, but as has been discussed in Chapter 2 this was a major cause of crony capitalism and the growth of black marketing and shortages in society.[169]

The OG 11 Percent Sarkar

The late Pakistani Prime Minister Benazir Bhutto's husband (and current President of that country) Asif Ali Zardari earned the derogatory nickname of "Mr Ten Percent" for his alleged practice of seeking 10 percent of the value of all contracts as bribes in lieu of granting government contracts.

In India, a southern Indian state government also earned this sobriquet from the opposition, albeit with a different percentage. But long-forgotten facts show that the latter was not the first in India to deserve this monicker. As early as 1964, the Santhanam Committee, set up by the Nehru Cabinet, reported that "there is a general impression that it is difficult to get things done without resorting to corruption." Giving and taking 7–11 percent of the contract value as bribes had become the norm and that

> in all contracts of construction, purchases, sales, and other regular business on behalf of the government a regular percentage is paid by the parties to the transaction and this is shared in agreed proportions" by the people making the decisions... In all cases failure to pay the percentage results in difficulties and delays in getting the bills paid.[170]

Continuing its indictment of the rising tide of crony capitalists and power brokers, the Santhanam Committee said:

> It is these persons who indulge in... avoidance of taxes, accumulate large amounts of unaccounted money by various methods such as obtaining licenses in the names of bogus firms and individuals, trafficking in licenses, suppressing profits by manipulation of accounts to avoid taxes... accepting money for transactions put through without accounting for it. It is they who maintain an army of liaison men and contact men, some of whom live, spend and entertain ostentatiously. We are unable to believe that so much money is being spent only for the purpose of getting things done quickly.[171]

The committee recorded its dismay at the all-pervasive corruption that was gnawing away at the innards of the state and which was fraying the sacred covenant between the rulers and the ruled. The report noted:

> It was represented to us that corruption has increased to such an extent that people have started losing faith in the integrity of public administration. We heard from all sides that corruption has, in recent years, spread even to those levels of administration from which it was conspicuously absent in the past. We wish we could confidently and without reservation assert that at the political level, ministers, legislators, party officials were free from this malady.[172]

No opposition leader could have put more succinctly or bluntly. It continued:

> The people of India rightly expected that, when the governance of the country passed into the hands of the disciples of the Father of the Nation who were in their own individual capacities known for high character and ability, governments in India, at the Centre and the States, would set up and achieve a standard of integrity, second to none in the world, both in the political and administrative aspects. It has to be frankly admitted that this hope has not been realized in full measure.[173]

Licensing Was the Root Cause of Corruption

It had been evident from the very beginning that the onerous and intrusive licensing and inspection system put in place by the government was not working and was, in fact, the root cause of India's continuing economic stagnation and rising corruption. The rules and regulations were designed to give the growing army of bureaucrats the power to manage the economy—a task for which they were not trained—and this soon degenerated into a new avenue for rent seeking.

In what was possibly the first serious official criticism of the government's licensing policies, the report recorded that

> the fact that licences worth Rs. 2,38,24,142 were obtained by fraud and other types of malpractices is a clear indication of the extent of the problem in the licensing activities of Government. It is common knowledge that each licence fetches anything between 100 per cent to 500 per cent of its face-value if sold. Thus, a huge unearned profit, which may be anything from Rupees two to ten crores, should have been made in these transactions and it is anybody's guess as to how much of it went into the pockets of public servants.[174]

Several nations, which had enacted laws to regulate and control their businesses during the Second World War, began to withdraw these restrictions after the War. India was an outlier and did not reduce oversight powers after the War. Rather, the Nehru government and its successors kept adding layers of regulation and supervision to already heavy doses of government control, effectively squeezing the spirit of innovation and risk-taking that are the lifeblood of business.

Under the sub-heading "Governments' taking upon themselves more than they can manage by way of regulatory functions," the report said:

> We are not in a position to assess the correctness of this criticism. But it is to be recognised that in all the fields where Government interferes to regulate and control there is scope for abuse. While it is not possible to accept the proposition that Government should divest itself of all regulatory functions and powers of control, it appears that it would be desirable. for each Ministry/Department to undertake a review of the regulatory functions which are

> its responsibility and also examine whether all of them are necessary and whether the manner of discharge of those functions and of the exercise of powers of control are capable of improvement. We recommend that such a review be made.[175]

Ministers Fail the Integrity Test

The committee also found that in some of Nehru's ministerial colleagues as well as among politicians who held high offices in the states, the idealism of the freedom movement had been replaced by an unhealthy craving for self-aggrandisement. It said:

> there is a widespread impression that failure of integrity is not uncommon among Ministers and that some Ministers who have held office during the last 16 years have enriched themselves illegitimately, obtained good jobs for their sons and relations through nepotism, and have reaped other advantages inconsistent with any notion of purity in public life. The general belief about failure of integrity amongst Ministers is as damaging as actual failure. That these Ministers have held office in the name of the Indian National Congress which had evolved the highest notions of personal integrity and service under the inspiration of Mahatma Gandhi has given rise to an exaggerated view of their failure to maintain high standards of integrity. It is a pity that neither the Congress authorities nor the great leaders who took over the Government of India realised the importance of evolving a suitable machinery and procedure for preventing and dealing with such corruption.[176]

This clearly shows that there was a considerable and lamentable laxity in the Nehru regime's oversight mechanism and supervisory functions. As the head of the administration, the Prime Minister has to bear responsibility for this lapse. It has to be reiterated once again that he could not have been completely oblivious to what was going on around him and so, will have to carry the cross for not leveraging his own reputation for probity and his personal political capital to bring his corrupt colleagues to book.

Further, despite all the tall talk of socialism, egalitarianism, honesty, and high decibel rhetoric on throwing black marketeers into jail, the stark reality was that the Nehruvian regime had presided over a period of unprecedented spread of unaccounted wealth and corruption. Ruing the spread of black money, the committee stated:

> To buy and sell properties at prices much greater than those recorded in the conveyance deeds has become a common method of cheating the Central Government of income-tax and other taxes and the State Government of the stamp duty and as a convenient method of transferring black money. If, in some manner, the Central and State Governments, or some special corporations set up for the purpose can be empowered to step in and acquire such properties at the stated value, or even at a small premium when it is considered that the properties have been deliberately under-valued, it will strike a blow against black money.
>
> Similarly, the habit of charging "pugri" or "premium" for renting houses and flats is a similar source of corruption for which some drastic steps have to be taken. We understand that this illegal "pugri" is taken not only by the owners of houses and flats, but also by the tenants who continue to hold on to them nominally and sublet to others.[177]

The committee identified broadly eight types of corruption that were widely prevalent:

1. Offences calculated to prevent or obstruct the economic development of the country and endanger its economic health;
2. Evasion and avoidance of taxes lawfully imposed;
3. Misuse of their position by public servants in making of contracts and disposal of public property, issue of licences and permits and similar other matters;
4. Delivery by individuals and industrial and commercial undertakings of goods not in accordance with agreed specifications in fulfilment of contracts entered into with public authorities;
5. Profiteering, black-marketing and hoarding;
6. Adulteration of foodstuffs and drugs;
7. Theft and misappropriation of public property and funds; and
8. Trafficking in licences, permits, etc.[178]

The report also recommended the means of curbing corruption:

> Specific allegation of corruption on the part of a Minister at the Centre or a State should be promptly investigated by an agency whose findings will command respect. We recognise that irresponsible allegations cannot be taken serious note of. We, therefore, suggest that if a formal allegation is made by any 10 Members of Parliament or a Legislature in writing addressed to the Prime Minister or Chief Minister, through the Speakers and Chairman, the Prime Minister or Chief Minister should consider himself obliged, by convention, to refer the allegations

> for immediate investigation by a Committee as has been suggested later in this Section.... This would be in addition to the responsibilities of the Prime Minister and Chief Ministers of States to take note of allegations made in the Press or which otherwise come to their notice.[179]

Then, as now, funding political parties was a major source of corruption, and the committee did not shy away from acknowledging it.

> The public belief in the prevalence of corruption at high political levels has been strengthened by the manner in which funds are collected by political parties, especially at the time of elections. Such suspicions attach not only to the ruling party but to all parties, as often the opposition can also support private vested interests as much as members of the Government party. It is, therefore, essential that the conduct of political parties should be regulated in this matter by strict principles in relation to collection of funds and electioneering.
>
> It has to be frankly recognised that political parties cannot be run and elections cannot be fought without large funds. But these funds should come openly from the supporters or sympathisers of the parties' concerned. If even one family in three pays one rupee a year to a political party, the total annual contribution will be more than what is needed for all legitimate purposes of all political parties in India. It is the reluctance and inability of these parties to make small collections on a wide basis and the desire to resort to short cuts through large donations that constitutes the major source of corruption and even more of suspicion of corruption.[180]

Chilling Effect on Free Speech

All the good work of the Santhanam Committee was considerably diluted by one dangerous suggestion. Though ostensibly aimed at curbing corruption in public life, it hid, in plain sight, phraseology that gave wide latitude to the political leadership of the day to interpret and misuse its provisions to crack down on media that exposed corruption in high places.

It said:

> While responsible newspapers should thus be encouraged to assist the public against corrupt officials, drastic action should be taken against irresponsible newspapers which make reckless allegations. It should become an invariable practice to prosecute such newspapers unless they can establish the truth of their allegations. It should not be left to individual officers or Ministers to take such action. The existing law and procedure will have to be reviewed from this point of view.[181]

Quod erat demonstrandum (QED)!

How the Nehruvian System Corrupted India

The Santhanam Committee report exposed the rot that had set in over Nehru's long and eventful reign. The government accepted 106 out its 137 recommendations. Yet, there was little material improvement in the quality of governance, and, after a brief interregnum during the Shastri years, corruption levels shot through the roof under the Prime Ministership of his successor, Indira Gandhi.

My parents and uncles would often narrate stories on the integrity of and genuine respect commanded by members of the Indian Civil Service and Imperial Police, the predecessors, respectively, of the Indian Administrative Service and the Indian Police Service. These people were mostly Indian—at least the ones my parents and uncles interacted closely with were—and all of them had reputations that were beyond reproach. These were the same officers from the same services who manned the upper reaches of the administration in the decade-and-a-half after Independence (IAS and IPS officers still had not gained the required seniority to be appointed Secretaries and heads of state police forces).

Then, what changed?

The difference was the multiplication of restrictions on setting up, expanding, and shutting down businesses. The difference also lay in the licensing of normal, everyday activities like buying cement for building a house. In this prevailing situation of overweening controls and shortages, various levels of officialdom were given discretionary powers to grant permits and licenses for economic activity as well as the purchase of scarce "canalized" items like cement and a few other items.

After Independence, the government recruited a huge army of lower-level bureaucrats to man the scaffolding of the wall of controls it set up to control all economic activity in the country as we have seen in Chapter 2. These government servants were poorly paid but were given the power to stall and even scuttle projects worth hundreds of crores by sitting on or refusing regular permissions.

In no time, the more enterprising and less honest among them began trading their signatures on permits for money. With many ministers and chief ministers also doing the same, as was noted by the Santhanam Committee, the senior bureaucracy in the middle soon found itself sandwiched between two powerful layers of corruption. It was just a matter of time before many of them, too, succumbed to the rising tide of dishonesty that has become a leitmotif of public life in India.

The Shastri Interregnum

Lal Bahadur Shastri succeeded Nehru as Prime Minister, and, although he set out to pull India out of the *cul-de-sac* his predecessor's policies had driven the country into, his reign was too short to make a marked difference to the environment of corruption that pervaded Indian public life. Yet, he did force his finance minister T.T. Krishnamachari, who had been a Nehru favourite, to resign when eleven MPs accused his relatives of amassing enormous wealth on the strength of his name and prestige.

Indira Gandhi Throws All Norms to the Wind

Indira Gandhi's long reign, in two stints, inflicted large-scale and lasting damage to India's democratic polity. Her policy of pursuing power at all costs, cutting corners, breaking norms and brazenly promoting her family further weakened the already fragile system of checks and balances that kept the wheels of governance moving. Result: democracy suffered; health, education, sanitation and people's welfare were neglected; cities degenerated into unplanned urban sprawls at the mercy of real estate sharks; and the moral compass of Indian politics hit rock bottom. Rampant corruption became the order of the day and, as in Nehru's time, went unpunished if the perpetrators were powerful and well connected.

With norms breaking down, the economy stagnating at the Nehruvian rate of growth, and corruption everywhere, jobs became increasingly scarce and youth increasingly frustrated at the lack of opportunities. A little over two decades after India's first Prime Minister decided to usher in a socialist pattern of society, the country was in turmoil. The hopelessness of the educated unemployed youth found expression in the highly misguided Naxalite movement in urban West Bengal. After a few years of endemic violence, the so-called revolution was crushed by brutal police action. The immediate danger to the Indian state had passed, but the underlying anger that had fuelled it continued to simmer just under the surface.

India's greatest filmmaker Satyajit Ray, who made his famous Calcutta Trilogy—*Pratidwandi*, *Jana Aranya*, and *Sheemaboddho*—captured the angst of the urban youth of the time. "I felt corruption, rampant corruption, all around," Ray said in 1982.[182]

The problem was multi-fold. India's socialist controls and the restrictions on growth severely constrained the ability of the economy to generate gainful employment for the huge army of workers that was joining the workforce every year. This was overlaid with corruption that had spread to every sphere of economic and social behaviour. There was a scarcity of almost everything, a thriving black market, and high prices all around.

Frustrated at every step, common Indians found a release in the adventures of the ubiquitous Vijay, the name usually given to Amitabh Bachchan's characters in a series of "Angry Young Man" movies in which the protagonist, who has usually suffered grave injustice at the hands of a corrupt, uncaring society as a child, grows up to become rich by hook or by crook—often on the wrong side of the law—and takes revenge on his tormentors. It was almost as if the audience was cheering for Vijay and living out his life as the vigilante justice giver as a balm for their own dreary existence.

This angst was understandable. There was barely any increase in the pool of people employed by the private sector, which stagnated at about 6.8 million in the four years between 1973 and 1977. The public sector, however, did take in additional people—the number of employees increased from 12 million to 14 million. Given that India's population increased by 57 million over this period, a vast majority of job seekers were forced to join the agricultural workforce or the unorganised sector.

Indira Gandhi's son, Sanjay Gandhi, did not have to worry about finding employment and was brazen about using his extra-constitutional powers. He held up an industrial license for petrochemical feedstock for Nusli Wadia, Chairman of Bombay Dyeing, as Wadia had refused to make a political donation. After his death, Rajiv Gandhi did help Wadia get the license, but the customs department held up his imported equipment for years, causing interminable delays in his project. Interestingly, the customs official who held up Wadia's machinery joined a rival company after retirement in a well-paying post-retirement sinecure.[183]

The Santhanam Committee had recommended that the Prime Minister should order an enquiry if credible allegations of corruption surfaced against senior ministers. But when Maharashtra chief minister A.R. Antulay, who was an Indira

Gandhi loyalist, began extorting corporate "donations" in lieu of supplies of cement, plots of land and industrial alcohol, allegedly to raise funds for charitable purposes, the committee's recommendations were ignored. The Prime Minister's blessings for this brazen act of corruption became evident when she inaugurated the Indira Gandhi Pratibha Pratishthan, one of the organisations set up by Antulay to accept the funds. When the public outrage became unbearable, she withdrew her name from the organisation and ordered Antulay to resign, but he was allowed to retain control of the funds he had raised.[184]

If this was not bad enough, Mrs Gandhi openly and blatantly seemed to justify corruption, saying it was a way of life and "a global phenomenon."[185] With such encouragement coming from the top, was it any surprise that corruption and bribery became endemic at every level of the government?

When Dishonesty Was Rewarded

In his beautifully written book *India Unbound*, Gurcharan Das mentioned how a neighbour in Chandigarh cheated his father out of his house by tricking him into mortgaging the property for a bank loan the neighbour needed to set up a malt unit that would supply feedstock to a brewery. Soon, the would-be entrepreneur was being hounded by the usual suspects for their cut: the bank manager wanted his share for the loan he had sanctioned; the factory inspector wanted his pound of flesh; the official from the electricity department refused to give a power connection unless he was compensated; the labour inspector and the excise department clerks wanted their share of the pie; and the minister threatened to change the rules to make it impossible for the entrepreneur to supply malt to the breweries unless he was paid his share.

It then emerged after a few years that the entrepreneur had actually siphoned off all the money from his company and turned it sick. The upshot of this was that the Das family lost their house, but the entrepreneur got away scot free. This is a typical example of how businessmen in India learned to game the system from the 1960s onwards by stripping their companies of assets and becoming rich, leaving lenders, employees, creditors and other stakeholders in the lurch. Hardly any such crooked entrepreneur ever went to jail.

Such was the atmosphere of impunity that Nehru's and Indira Gandhi's version of socialism had engendered in India.

Bans on Corporate Donations Institutionalised Corruption

Indira Gandhi banned corporate donations to political parties in 1969 ostensibly to fight corporate influence in politics, but most people believe there was a more sinister and less altruistic motive. But first some background:

The following is an excerpt from an article dated April 9, 2019, on the ORF website, titled "Financing Elections in India: A Scrutiny of Corporate Donation," by Niranjan Sahoo:

> The history of corporate funding of political parties in India goes back to the freedom movement. The Birlas were one of the leading donors of the Indian National Congress.
>
> After Independence, the business class as a whole secured some leverage over the shaping of the Congress government's economic policy. It contributed the majority of donations towards poll spending in the post-independence era. In the 1960s, the Congress and the Swatantra Party—the latter started by C. Rajagopalachari

> as a party advocating free enterprise —were the main beneficiaries of donations from big conglomerates such as the Tatas and the Birlas, who together accounted for 34 per cent of the total company contributions between 1962 and 1968.
>
> In 1969, the Indira Gandhi government imposed a complete ban on corporate funding (via deletion of the Section 293A of the Companies Act) to break the nexus between politics and businesses and also to check the popularity of the centre-right Swatantra Party by drying it off finances.
>
> However, this proved counterproductive. To beat the ban, political parties started raising funds by publishing souvenirs, in which advertisements were placed by the business houses. Businesses also resorted to tax evasions, black-market operations and other illegal mechanisms due to political compulsions and the threat of selective raids and nationalisation. This period also saw the rise of "briefcase politics" through which vast amounts of black money was transferred into the Congress Party account.
>
> In the era of license permit raj, this arrangement also suited the businesses. However, a forward-looking Rajiv Gandhi government, intending to end the culture of license permit raj, took a crucial decision of lifting the ban in 1985.[186]

Sahoo's article lays bare the corruption and the sleaze that had crept into governance under the watch of Indira Gandhi.

In June 1970, the Indira Gandhi government enacted the Monopolies and Restrictive Trade Practices (MRTP) Act. Like the ban on corporate donations, this move, too, was sold to the country as a socialist measure to curb the power of big industrialists. But, in practice, MRTP became yet another instrument with which the authorities could delay or scupper corporate expansions and diversifications. Permissions under MRTP, thus, became another source of rent seeking by influential politicians and bureaucrats.

Journalist and author Kuldip Nayar alleged that Mrs Gandhi was likely the final recipient of the briefcases and suitcases that made their way to the Congress party. Sadashiv Kanoji Patil, a member of the notorious Congress Syndicate, alleged in an interview to Nayar that he had given Mrs Gandhi a large sum of money and grumbled that she did not even return the suitcase.[187]

Banking Due Diligence Gets Diluted, Opens Floodgates for Loot

India's banking system began its climb down the steep and slippery slope of corruption, shoddy due diligence, and chronic bad loans during Indira Gandhi's reign. Her son Sanjay Gandhi's ambitions of building a fully indigenous car was approved by his mother's government by throwing several norms to the wind. A huge amount of land was acquired by the Haryana government and allotted to him at a very cheap price. Central Bank and Punjab National Bank, which had recently been nationalised by Indira Gandhi, were then arm twisted to advance loans to the fledgling company on very favourable terms. L.N. Mishra, a powerful minister in Mrs Gandhi's Cabinet, helped him raise funds "including by helping to collect large amounts as advances from the dealers who would sell the cars."[188]

This was the beginning of the decline in the credit quality of banks as influential people with political backing took loans that many of them did not ever repay, leaving banks with large amounts of non-performing assets, a euphemism for unpaid loans. As the integrity of the banking sector began to fray, its financial viability began to suffer.

Indira Gandhi did not lift a finger to stem this open loot. Economist I.G. Patel, who was Economic Affairs Secretary during her reign, said that she was consumed by "hubris and delusion… she could do what she liked and did not have to worry much about right and wrong." L.N. Mishra would frequently badger him "to favour some firm or another for obvious quid pro quo." It was obvious that Mishra, Sanjay Gandhi and his mother were in it all together.[189]

Corruption Permeates Every Aspect of Public Life

Sanjay Gandhi played a big role in engineering Mrs Gandhi's return to power in 1980. In that election, he gave tickets to about a hundred of his camp followers, many of whom became MPs. His storm troopers were very different from the previous generation of politicians, most of whom were *khadi* clad and had cut their teeth playing major or minor roles in the freedom struggle. The newer lot were more likely to wear safari suits and, according to Indira Gandhi's biographer Inder Malhotra, "looked upon their membership of Parliament and their proximity to the centre of power as a short-cut to making the maximum possible amount of money in the shortest period of time."[190]

Thus, the corruption and crony capitalism that were ushered in by Nehru's licensing policies were encouraged by his daughter. Indira Gandhi's long rule was not only an era of unbridled corruption but also, unfortunately, a period when corruption was institutionalised and imbued into the body of Indian public life.

8

Policy Mistakes That Kept India Poor

While India was lurching from crisis to crisis and its Prime Minister was going around the world begging for food and other aid to keep the country afloat, a tiny city state, which had once been part of India's sphere of influence and whose name was drawn from Sanskrit, was slowly and at first unsteadily, marking its journey as an independent nation. Today, that poverty-stricken and resourceless dot on the map is a First World country with a per capita income higher than that of most European countries.

In India, Nehru's legions of followers defend his track record by citing the enormity of the crises that confronted him at Independence. The truth is that every newly independent country in Asia faced similar challenges—of poverty, hunger, homelessness, lack of economic development, large-scale illiteracy, absence of resources, and the dubious attraction of communism or some form of socialism.

Singapore was faced with an existential crisis at birth. It became part of Malaysia but deep and fundamental disagreements with the government at Kuala Lumpur led to a second separation within two years.

Lee Kuan Yew Shows Singapore the Way

It was forced to leave the Malaysian Federation in particularly difficult circumstances. At the time of its independence in

August 1965, there were very real concerns about Singapore's prospects of survival. Singapore's legendary Prime Minister Lee Kuan Yew wrote in his memoir:

> We had been asked to leave Malaysia and go our own way with no signposts to our next destination. We faced tremendous odds with an improbable chance of survival... On that 9th day of August 1965, I started out with great trepidation on a journey along an unmarked road to an unknown destination.[191]

Ironically, Lee's role model for the development of his impoverished city state was reportedly Calcutta, then declining but still a major metropolis in Asia. But Calcutta's stars had already begun to wane with the rise of the communist movement, and the city was a pale shadow of its former self by the beginning of the 1970s.

Singapore's second Prime Minister Goh Chok Tong, who succeeded Lee in 1990, revealed the secret sauce of Singapore's success story very succinctly. Addressing ruling party workers on November 15, 1992, he said:

> During the recent Non-Aligned Meeting in Jakarta, the Nepalese Prime Minister asked me for the secret of Singapore's success. I smiled and replied, Lee Kuan Yew. I went on to explain that I meant it as a short form to encapsulate the principles, values and determination with which he governed and built Singapore.[192]

Lee's Success Mantras: Get Rid of Communists, Welcome MNCs

After coming to power in June 1959, the new Singapore government, like the Congress government in India 12 years previously, decided on a strategy of industrialisation to deal with the city state's declining entrepôt trade, high unemployment and absence of natural resources. In line with this goal, it sought the help of the United Nations, which sent a mission led by a Dutch economist Albert Winsemius to draw up an industrialisation programme for Singapore. Winsemius and his team of experts studied the situation and recommended a solution: "a crash programme to reduce unemployment and a 10-year programme to attract foreign investment to Singapore with appropriate incentives."[193]

Winsemius, however, had two caveats, which he said could preclude Singapore from achieving success. In order to reach its goals, the Dutch economist told Lee that he had to:

1. Get rid of the Communists. "How you get rid of them does not interest me as an economist, but get them out of the government, get them out of the unions, get them off the streets. How you do it, is your job," he said; and
2. "Let the statue of [Stamford] Raffles [who founded Singapore] stand where he stands today; say publicly that you accept the heavy ties with the West because you will very much need them in your economic programme."

Pragmatism Trumps Socialist Dogma

Like Nehru, Lee, too, was instinctively a socialist and very proud of his roots, but, unlike India's first Prime Minister, he was not dogmatic about the infallibility of his ideology. Choosing pragmatism over doctrinaire rigidity, Lee paid heed to Winsemius' advice. He ruthlessly crushed the communists and laid out the red carpet for multinational corporations from the US, Europe, and Japan.

Describing his approach to developing Singapore as "pragmatic," Lee said in 1998 that he was "prepared to look at the problem and say, all right, what is the best way to solve it that will produce the maximum happiness and well-being for the maximum number of people."[194]

In November 1993, speaking to a team of visiting African leaders, Lee advised them to adopt a pragmatic approach to formulating economic policies rather than a dogmatic stance. In the 1960s and 1970s, the zeitgeist was anti-American and anti-multinational corporations, but Lee consciously chose to swim against this tide. He "assiduously courted MNCs" because "they had the technology, know-how, techniques, expertise and the markets" and "it was a fast way of learning on the job working for them and with them." This strategy of relying on the MNCs paid off as "they have been a powerful factor in Singapore's growth." Lee firmly believed that Singapore succeeded because it "rejected conventional wisdom when it did not accord with rational analysis and his own experience."[195]

He elaborated on this in July 2009, in an interview to American journalist Tom Plate:

> I do not work on a theory. Instead, I ask: What will make this work? If, after a series of such solutions and I find that a certain approach worked, then I try to find out what was the principle behind the solution... What is my guiding principle? Presented with a difficulty or major problem or an assessment of conflicting facts, I review what alternatives I have if my proposed solution doesn't work. I choose a

> solution which offers a higher probability of success, but if it fails, I have some other way. Never a dead end.[196]

From the above, it will be evident that Lee adopted a pragmatic approach to policy formulation that involved "a willingness to introduce new policies or modify existing ones as circumstances dictate, regardless of ideological principles."[197]

India Goes the Other Way

Nehru's policies and those followed by his daughter Indira Gandhi were the diametrical opposite of those adopted by Lee. As we have seen, India's first Prime Minister hated the word "profit" and believed that the primary task of public sector companies was not to earn profits but to fulfil social responsibilities. "Nehru," writes Ramchandra Guha, "at once an Indian Brahmin, an English aristocrat, and a European social democrat naturally despised moneymaking, and, hence, the profit motive that usually drives private enterprise."[198]

As we have seen in previous chapters, India's first Prime Minister not only stood against the profit motive, but he also discouraged the private sector, considered businessmen to be dishonest and did not respect wealth creators. His government also actively discouraged foreign trade and foreign investments and walked the extra mile to make multinational corporations feel unwelcome.

Unlike Lee, who accepted the advice of Winsemius, Nehru chose to ignore the sage advice from the World Bank, IMF and several highly acclaimed economists who warned him that his policies were headed for failure.

Both Lee and Nehru were influenced by British Marxist economist, Labour Party politician and London School of Economics professor Harold Laski. But Lee obviously kept in mind how several of Laski's students had achieved power in their home countries and then run their economies into quicksand by following their teacher's "socialist theories." He also learnt the right lessons from the colossal failures of Nehru's socialist policies, which Nehru himself did not. "It was my good fortune that I had several of these failed economies to warn me of this danger before I was in a position to do any harm in government," Lee said many years later.[199]

In 2013, Lee praised economics Nobel Prize winner Friedrich Hayek as "a very clear thinker" who "hit upon the eternal truth, explaining that the free market is necessary to get the economy right." That same year he also wrote: "Long before Milton Friedman held up Hong Kong as a model of a free enterprise economy, I had seen the advantage of having little or no social safety net." Contrary to popular belief, Singapore is not a welfare state. People pay for healthcare and pensions from their savings, but since taxes are low, they are able to save a lot.

Reading Lee's recollections about his management style, one cannot help wondering how different India's development trajectory could have been had Nehru displayed similar vision and pragmatism and, like Lee, endeavoured to "have another way," instead of leading the Indian economy into a dead end. It had become evident within one year of launching the Second Five Year Plan—and definitely by its end—that it was not working and that the growth and other developmental goals would fall way short of targets.

Several Indian and international experts had also identified the shortcomings of the Plan. Yet, Nehru and his advisors seemed to have allowed hubris, dogma and ideological blinkers to reign and ignored all advice that warned of the dangers ahead. Far from changing course, they went full steam ahead with their development agenda. The results are there for everyone to see.

In 1991, when India was belatedly changing course and correcting the policy mistakes of the past, Singapore, which had started out at roughly the same level as India in 1965, had marched far ahead on the strength of its pragmatic policies followed by its visionary leader. World Bank data shows that both Singapore and India were in the throes of abject poverty in 1965—when Singapore began its journey as an independent nation and India had been free of colonial rule for 18 years.

Singapore then had a per capita income of $516.5,[200] which was 4.25 times the comparable figure of $121.5 in India.[201] In 1991, the gap had widened beyond recognition. Singapore's per capita income had soared to $14,502.38, which was an incredible 47.46 times India's figure of $305.6. In the 26 years since Singapore's independence, its per capita income had grown 28.07 times. Indians had multiplied their income only 2.52 times.

In 1991, the Indian exchequer was almost bankrupt and Indians still struggled with abject poverty, while Singapore had become rich and was becoming richer. The geometric progression of income levels in Singapore was also accompanied by a drastic decline in unemployment from 14 percent to 2.1 percent between 1959 and 2016 for which figures are available.

Lee Displays Exemplary, Visionary Leadership

In his memoirs, Lee emphasised the importance of good leadership. He wrote:

> My experience of developments in Asia has led me to conclude that we need good men to have good government. However good the system of government, bad leaders will bring harm to their people. ... The single decisive factor that made for Singapore's development was the ability of its ministers and the high quality of the civil servants who supported them. Indeed, leaders matter because of their role in "stretching" the constraints of "geography and natural resources, institutional legacies and international location."[202]

Singapore faced several Himalayan constraints in its development journey—geography, resources, manpower, and education. It is only in the face of adversity that a leader's mettle is tested. On this, Lee and his team displayed exceptional leadership and management skills and succeeded in overcoming the constraints and transformed Singapore to First World status by 2000.

In the same speech, referred to above, Goh asserted that meritocracy was the key to Singapore's success because the "practice of meritocracy in the civil service, in politics, in business and in schools" enabled Singaporeans "to achieve excellence and to compete against others."

Lee Nips Corruption in the Bud; Nehru, Indira Look the Other Way

Another major challenge that Lee had to overcome was all-pervasive corruption. Lee wrote in his memoirs:

> We were sickened by the greed, corruption and decadence of many Asian leaders... We had a deep sense of mission to establish a clean and effective government. When we took the oath of office... in June 1959, we all wore white shirts

> and white slacks to symbolise purity and honesty in our personal behaviour and our public life... We made sure from the day we took office in June 1959 that every dollar in revenue would be properly accounted for and would reach the beneficiaries at the grass roots as one dollar, without being siphoned off along the way. So, from the very beginning we gave special attention to the areas where discretionary powers had been exploited for personal gain and sharpened the instruments that could prevent, detect or deter such practices.[203]

The strict and impartial enforcement of the Prevention of Corruption Act (POCA) by the Corrupt Practices Prevention Bureau (CPIB) has resulted in corruption being virtually stamped out in Singapore, which is among the least corrupt countries in Asia, according to Transparency International's Corruption Perception Index.

We have seen in the previous chapter how unreasonable restrictions on normal business activities and discretionary powers bestowed on various levels of political and bureaucratic authorities forced even honest people to cut corners and resort to corrupt practices. Like Lee, both Nehru and his daughter stood heads and shoulders above everyone else in the government. Had they so desired, they could have cracked down on corruption and put a halt to the kleptocracy that was developing across the length and breadth of the government and then spreading across society like a wildfire. But they, purposely or otherwise, chose to follow the example of Gandhiji's three monkeys and saw no evil being perpetrated, heard nothing, and spoke little about it except in rhetorical terms.

Communists Get a Free Pass in India

Unlike Lee, Nehru and his daughter gave a free pass to communist intellectuals. Being a committed socialist, it was natural that Nehru would heed the advice from his fellow travellers. He also remained sympathetic to communists till the end of his life. On his return from a Commonwealth Conference in London in 1948, he wrote to Sardar Patel that "even Lady Mountbatten was worried about" and "Members of the Parliament spoke about" Patel's crackdown on communist leaders.[204]

It can be said in Nehru's defence that he did not have Lee's example to follow. His daughter Indira Gandhi cannot hide behind the same excuse. When she came to power in 1966, Lee had already set Singapore on the path to growth. She also had the examples of South Korea, Taiwan and Hong Kong to follow.

Leftward Lurch Squeezes All Life Out of the Economy

Indira Gandhi took the Indian economy much further left than even her father did. She also strengthened the straitjacket that was already squeezing the lifeblood out of Indian entrepreneurship. She could have followed Lee's example of cracking down on the communists and encouraging multinational corporations, but, instead, she went headlong in the opposite direction.

Politically dependent on the CPI and CPI(M) from November 1969 till March 1971 for the survival of her minority government following the split in the Indian National Congress, Mrs Gandhi embarked on a series of policy measures to burnish her own socialist credentials. The easiest and cheapest way to do so and appear pro-poor in India was to soak the rich and adopt a stringent anti-business stance.

She appointed communist economist Dr Ashok Mitra as Chief Economic Advisor in 1970. Her close advisor P.N. Haksar—who strongly advocated for social control over banks, nationalisation of insurance, strict control over imports and exports, state trading in food grains, consumer co-ops, control over monopolies, focus on minimum needs, urban land ceiling, land reforms in rural areas, and abolition of privileges, titles and privy purses to the former rulers—was known for his strong views in favour socialism. He is believed to have been the brain behind her emotional call to eradicate poverty—*Garibi Hatao*. All his other pet themes mentioned above also found their way into the government's policies. Mrs Gandhi then raised the marginal rate of income tax to 97.5 percent.

Whether these measures helped the poor is doubtful. There was little visible manifestation of a dramatic improvement in their welfare and even less evidence to prove their effectiveness in achieving even a partial uplift of their living standards. In other words, the poor remained where they had been before. But the propaganda surrounding her "pro-poor" policies sealed her image as a messiah of the downtrodden. They also set back the Indian economy and the country's development trajectory by decades even as the rest of Asia were racing ahead on the path of capitalist development. The low hanging fruits that could still be plucked to race up the development ladder were fast being consumed by India's South East Asian peers. Soon, there would be none left for India.

Mrs Gandhi was too well travelled, cosmopolitan and well connected to the global intellectual elite not to have known that her policies were setting India on the path to economic oblivion, but, by then, consolidation of all power in her own person was all that mattered to her.

If India missed the bus in the 1950s and early 1960s because of Nehru's stubborn refusal to take off his ideological blinkers, the nation again missed the train in the 1970s and early 1980s because of his daughter's reluctance to shed her inherited ideological fetters. The big loser on both occasions was the Indian population that had entrusted their future in the custody of their chosen leaders.

She also appointed Marxist-leaning academic Sayyid Nurul Hasan—ironically, the son-in-law of an until-recently reigning 15-gun-salute Nawab—as Education Minister in 1972 and effectively handed over the reins of Indian academia to a crop of Marxist scholars and intellectuals. Soon, all Indian educational institutions, think tanks, large NGOs, the foreign ministry, the finance ministry, the culture ministry and all their affiliated bodies were awash with Marxist intellectuals and their fellow travellers. Given the ideological leanings of her advisors, it was natural that Mrs Gandhi's policies reflected the biases of her core team. They, in turn, hardwired their ideology into several generations of Indians by indoctrinating them via their vice-like grip over school and college curricula, mass media, and even some entertainment platforms.

Indira Turns Away Foreign Investments

Unlike Lee, who was willing to learn from his own mistakes and those of other failed Asian leaders, Mrs Gandhi went much further than even her father to discourage foreign investments. She enacted the Foreign Exchange Regulation Act 1973, which made it mandatory for multinational corporations to divest stakes in their Indian subsidiaries beyond 40 percent within two years.

One of the most important aspects of Lee's development model was to attract foreign investment by assuring them of strong property rights. This enabled Singapore to actively woo multinational corporations. But Mrs Gandhi's hostility towards them was a blunt way of declaring that foreign investments were unwelcome in India.

Following Mrs Gandhi's defeat and the rise to power of the newly formed Janata Party, there was a brief period of hope that India might, at last, embark on a new set of pragmatic economic policies. But any residual hopes in this regard were belied when the government of Morarji Desai used the FERA law to force IBM and Coca-Cola to leave the country. Neither was ready to risk its patents in a regime where they did not own a majority stake in their Indian subsidiary. Since the Indian government was not willing to make an exception for them, they chose to leave. The new government's anti-business messaging got worse when it summarily sacked the highly respected J.R.D. Tata as Chairman of the public sector Air India.

Honest, Accountable Governance

Lee's multifaceted genius for public administration comes through in his success in ensuring honest and accountable governance. From the very beginning, he knew that he had to pay government servants and ministers competitive, market-linked salaries and perquisites if he wanted to attract the brightest minds. But initially, he could not afford to pay them at par with the private sector. So, he focused on imposing strong punitive punishments on those who strayed from the straight and narrow path. But he corrected the salaries of his ministerial colleagues and career bureaucrats to the highest levels in the world as soon as he could afford to.

But governance in Singapore does not depend only on high salaries and punitive punishments that include dismissal from service in extreme cases. It incentivises performance by removing the relationship between positions and age. In Singapore, for instance, "headmasters are often appointed in their 30s and rewarded with merit pay if they do well but are moved on quickly if their schools underperform."[205]

Ability to Take Advantage of International Developments

Singapore's ascent to the global high table was enabled by Lee's uncanny knack of being able to read international developments and ride global financial upheavals to take his city state a notch higher. In 1971, when the US delinked the dollar from gold, Lee read the situation better than most others, anticipated where the world was headed, and grasped the opportunity with both hands to establish Singapore as a regional centre for foreign exchange. This helped place Singapore as one of the world's great financial centres and a hub of global commerce.

He also set up the Housing Development Board and Economic Development Board, which transformed the severely space-constrained tiny island into one of the world's leading metropolises. It was his foresight and planning that enabled Singaporeans to come out of their ghettos into well planned mixed townships and provided what is arguably among the world's best living conditions for its citizens.

India, under Nehru and then Indira Gandhi, on the other hand, missed no opportunity to miss an opportunity offered by favourable international developments. We have seen in previous chapters how India missed the opportunity to ride the two-decades-long boom in international trade following the Second World War because of Nehru's conflation of export competitiveness with imperialism. India, thus, lost the chance of being an early bird and becoming part of the international value chain. It lost a similar chance once again under Indira in the 1970s and 1980s, when conditions again favoured such a development. Millions of Indians lost the chance of a better future because of these failures by India's leaders to take advantage of propitious global tailwinds.

Slums Proliferate in India

At the time of Independence, Singapore, Calcutta and Bombay ranked among the great metropolises of Asia and several other Indian cities like New Delhi, Bangalore, Chennai, and Hyderabad, among others, were considered very liveable cities. In the decades since then, Singapore has become part of the First World, Calcutta has fallen off the global map of great cities, while Mumbai and Delhi rank among the most congested, polluted and least liveable cities in the world.[206]

An unfortunate side effect of rapid urbanisation in India has been the proliferation of slum clusters in all the major cities. The genesis of this can also be traced back to Nehru's insistence on centrally planning every aspect of India's economic development. As a result, once charming cities developed slum clusters where mostly migrants and the poor eked out their existence in appallingly poor sanitary surroundings.

The failure began with Nehru's rejection of the Wage Goods Model of development and his adoption of the Temples of Modern India strategy, which placed all his eggs in the heavy industries basket. This capital-intensive model of growth in a labour-rich country failed to generate jobs and left millions of young Indians unemployed. The absence of any plan to provide basic education on a mass scale left them unprepared for employment. With rural India offering no scope for survival, these people started migrating to cities in search of livelihoods. They lived in abandoned pipes, flimsy sheds, and bamboo and burlap shanties they built on vacant parcels of land. In no time, these mushroomed into slums.

Unlike Singapore, where Lee provided government housing for everyone, Nehru's central planning made no provisions for these migrants. Even if he had, there were not enough resources to house them all in the cities. Decentralised development and the setting up of small-scale industry clusters in different parts of the country should have been the answer to this problem. Multiple birds could have been killed with this one stone—employment, education, housing, demand creation, and overall economic development.

Singapore and Lee nailed it; Nehru and his planners failed to implement something similar in India. This resulted in all-round failure and the development of slums across urban India.

Nehru's Belief in Scientific Planning Belied

In 1959, Nehru reiterated his determination to stay the

course. Speaking to Russi Karanjia of the *Blitz*, he said that his industrialisation programme was about to gather momentum and become a "self-feeding, self-propelling, and self-developing" phenomenon. Quite incredibly, he insisted that India had chosen "a scientific approach" to development, which was driven by a "mathematical formula." He added that subject to the "quality of the human being" and "climate and other factors," "planning and development have become a sort of mathematical formula, which may be worked out scientifically. If you do this, this is bound to follow, and this is going to be the next step and that [leads to] the third step."[207]

His simplistic faith in this cause-and-effect formula was a serious mistake, as it made him believe that his industrialisation programme was working even though he did accept that progress in agriculture was "disappointing." However, he brushed off any responsibility for this failure by blaming this lack of progress on "bad harvests, bad this and that," as well as peasants who were imbued with "orthodoxy and customs."[208]

These beliefs made him oblivious to the failure of the Second Plan. So, instead of correcting the failures of the Plan, the Third Plan was a scaled-up version of the Second Plan. The allocation for agriculture remained the same despite Nehru's disappointment with the progress of the sector in the Second Plan.

Three generations of Indians would have to pay a very heavy price for his ideological dogma and his egoistic refusal to accept his mistake.

Dirigiste Dogma

There was a broad consensus in the early and middle decades of the twentieth century that strong, state-led development that privileged the public sector over private capital and initiative was the way forward. Indian-born British liberal economist, author, professor and consultant, Deepak Lall, best known for his 1983 book *The Poverty of Development Economics*, calls this school of thinking "dirigiste dogma." Broadly, this school advocates massive government intervention as a substitute for market mechanisms to decide asset and resource allocations, because it believes that classical liberal economic theories on free trade are not suitable for the developing world. This school of thought theorised that the market would not be able to address the problems of poverty and human development and so needed the government to redistribute wealth through massive price and wage controls. They coined fancy terms like "unequal terms of trade," "foreign exchange bottlenecks," "basic needs" etc. and, on this basis, created policies for destitute people. The poor were used as guinea pigs. For example, in India, politicians and economists lurched from policy to policy in search of a balm for the condition even as liberal economics was lifting millions of people to higher standards of living in East and South East Asia.

In her beautifully written book *Durbar*, Tavleen Singh recounted her visit to Rae Bareli, Indira Gandhi's constituency, in 1979, on the trail of Rajmata Vijaya Raje Scindia's campaign against the then former Prime Minister. More than three decades after Independence, the road leading to the VIP constituency was marked by the absence of tarmac and her car "lurched from one rubble-filled ditch to the next, raising such a large cloud of dust that"[209] she and her co-passengers had to roll up the windows.

As they passed the villages in the constituency, they noticed women wearing tattered sarees; the children looked dirty and were "naked... with protruding bellies."[210] She noticed their "hair was bleached from malnutrition," as they played near their mothers. "I remember thinking, but surely Mrs Gandhi's constituency should have looked better," Singh wrote incredulously. Rae Bareli could well have been the template for any of India's more than 6.5 lakh villages. The villagers, she soon discovered, did not have electricity, drinking water, or even water for their fields.[211]

This pointed to a massive failure of both policy and planning in the 33 years since the departure of the British.

Incidentally, at the time of Independence, India had an installed electricity capacity of 1,362 MW and a per capita consumption of 16 kWh. In 1950, only 3,061 out of more than 6.5 lakh villages were electrified. In 1990, at the end of the Seventh Five Year Plan, these figures had risen to 63,636 MW with a per capita consumption of 329 kWh. The number of electrified villages had crawled up to 4,70,838 or only 70 percent of India's villages had electricity connections.[212] That means 30 percent of Indian villages, numbering about 1,95,000 villages, still had no access to electricity.

Other Policies That Stifled Growth and Hobbled Wealth Creation

As we said in Chapter 6, it is sound and rational systems and law that enable a country to march forward. In the sphere of economic activities, one will notice that all the countries that are rich, have competitive industries, own big brands and enjoy high standards of living have a few things in common. All of them have laws that encourage the private sector, reasonable tax rates (at least for the middle classes, to allow for high savings and investment rates), low rates of corruption, close to 100 percent literacy, high standards of health, education and sanitation, and a state apparatus that ensures the rule of law for the common man.

Almost all the economic policy interventions of the socialist state in India were heavy handed and ham fisted and were designed to curb economic activity and encourage rent seeking behaviour by authorities with great discretionary powers. They were also tailored to stifle innovation, competition and initiative. Instead of encouraging risk-taking and entrepreneurship, they were devised to benefit only the best-connected, the corrupt, and the speculators.

The basis—the root cause—of India's inability to progress at par with her Asian neighbours was socialism. It was not just a mistake; it was a blunder of Himalayan proportions to have selected socialism as the bedrock of India's economic policy. Empirical evidence proves that this philosophy has not been able to deliver lasting and high levels of economic growth anywhere in the world, although it did enable Eastern Europe and Cuba to attain high scores on almost every social indicator. Thirty-four years after abandoning Nehruvian socialism, India has still not recovered fully from the deleterious effects of this philosophy, which continues to exercise its hold over the psyche of an influential section of the old elite.

In the previous chapters and preceding passages, we have already mentioned licensing, privileging the public sector over private players, MRTP, FERA, import restrictions, and some other policies and laws that stifled growth and prevented employment generation.

There were several others that were equally, if not more, detrimental to the well-being of the Indian economy. Listing all of them would require an encyclopedia. The following are some of the most striking examples of policy mistakes by Indian planners:

- **Freight Equalisation Policy:**
  Location is considered one of the most important attributes of a business. Traditionally, industries came up near the sources of raw materials. Over time, these areas developed into industrial clusters as more companies and their ancillary, feeder, and downstream units came up in close proximity to the mother plant. For example, the Ruhr region in Germany is rich in natural resources such as iron ore, coal, lead, salt, and zinc. That is a major reason for its development as a major industrial centre in Europe.

  Similarly, the presence of iron and coal mines in Jharkhand, West Bengal, and Odisha led to the development of the industrial townships of Jamshedpur, Durgapur and Asansol, which supported the establishment of steel plants, their associate companies and a large foundry and engineering industry in the area.

  The attraction for the entrepreneurs: easy availability of raw materials and cheap transportation costs.

In 1952, the Nehru government implemented the Freight Equalisation Policy. Its stated goal was to facilitate the equal growth of industry all over India. This was among the first of many bureaucratic interventions in the workings of the market and was designed to neutralise the natural competitive advantage of location. A factory could be set up anywhere in the country, and the transportation of minerals would be subsidised by the government.

This policy, which was extant till 1993, set back the development trajectory of the mineral-rich eastern and central Indian states of West Bengal, Jharkhand (Bihar), Odisha, Assam, Madhya Pradesh and Chhattisgarh by nullifying their locational advantage. Transportation costs would remain the same for private and public sector companies whether they set up their processing units in close proximity to the mines or a thousand miles away. As a result of this policy, business houses began setting up their factories in coastal states like Maharashtra, Tamil, Nadu, Andhra Pradesh, Karnataka, and Gujarat, and large markets such as Bombay, Delhi, Bangalore, Hyderabad, Pune, and Ahmedabad. Therefore, heavy and middle industries began to develop far away from the sources of raw materials.

This has been criticised for promoting unequal growth—the exact opposite outcome of the stated goal of the policy—by depriving the poor eastern states of the benefits of industrial development. A July 2018 study by John Firth of CGD and Notre Dame and Earnest Liu of Princeton University titled

"Manufacturing Underdevelopment: India's Freight Equalisation Scheme, and the Long-run Effects of Distortions on the Geography of Production"[213] found "that over the long-run… [the policy] contributed to the decline of industry in eastern India, pushing iron and steel using industries towards more prosperous states. This effect sinks in gradually, however, with the time needed to construct new plants."

The repeal of the Freight Equalisation Policy did not restore the natural locational advantage of the eastern states by encouraging the setting up of processing industries close to the mines. One possible reason for this is the development of industry clusters in the states where the mother plants were set up. Reason: it would be too expensive and cumbersome to replicate the infrastructure from scratch in the eastern states.

However, Odisha has partially overcome this constraint by encouraging large private investors to set up iron and steel factories and related industries in the state.

- **Treating telephones as a luxury item:**

  India had a tele-density of 0.02 percent in March 1948. In March 1991, on the eve of the liberalisation of the Indian economy, this figure had crawled up to 0.60 percent.[214] Forty-four years after Independence, only six out of 1,000 Indians had telephone connections.

  Till 1995, telecom was a government monopoly and suffered all the negatives associated with government ownership of any asset. As the figures above show, tele-density had barely crawled up in the 44 years since Independence. That is because the government and the bureaucrats who managed the sector considered telecom to be a luxury and, therefore, unworthy of anything more than only cursory attention.

Since the 1980s, there had been a mini-revolution in the proliferation of PCO booths across the country—in *paan* shops, *kirana* shops, snack bars, other retail stores, and at standalone phone booths. This meant many more Indians were using phones to make calls but a personal phone connection was still a faraway dream for most.

As subsequent developments proved, the opportunity cost of the bureaucratic lethargy and political shortsightedness in ignoring the telecom sector was massive and was a huge drag on the country's development trajectory. That is because the telephony sector, like electricity and transportation, is an enabler of almost every other stream of economic activity. An efficient telecom network is, therefore, a necessary precondition for overall economic growth and individual economic uplift.

By treating this essential infrastructure as a luxury, India's rulers made a mistake and set back the possibility of a growth spurt by several years.

- **Controller of Capital Issues:**

Before the establishment of the Securities and Exchange Board of India (SEBI), capital issues were governed by the Controller of Capital Issues (CCI), under the provisions of the Capital Issues (Control) Act, 1947.

The Act's objectives were:[215]

(i) to ensure that investment in the private corporate sector does not violate priorities and objectives laid down in the Five Year Plans or flow into unproductive sectors;

(ii) to promote the expansion of private corporate sector on sound lines in general, and further the growth of particular corporate enterprises having sound capital structure; and

(iii) to distribute capital issues time-wise in such a manner that there is no overcrowding in a particular period.

In keeping with the government's goal of keeping the private sector in check, it arrogated to itself the right to decide which company could raise how much money at what price. This went against the grain of the very basis of the philosophy of stock markets.

The Act said: No company shall, "except with the consent of the Central Government, make an issue of capital."[216]

These powers made the CCI a major arbiter of speculation on the stock market. Since every issue was floated at prices way below their intrinsic value and almost invariably listed at a large premium to the offer price, IPOs became lottery tickets in the hands of allottees. Promoters and other insiders took advantage of this to earn huge amounts of speculative profits. Like licenses and permits, the office of CCI became another node in the body of the rent-seeking bureaucracy. The artificially low offer prices approved by the CCI meant that companies did not get the best prices for their fundamentals. This rendered the entire process inefficient and left room for corrupt practices that worked to the detriment of non-promoter shareholders.

With the liberalisation of the Indian economy in 1991, the CCI was scrapped on August 5, 1992, and replaced by SEBI, which has since regulated the stock market.

- **The Urban Land (Ceiling and Regulation) Act 1976**:

This was yet another law passed by the Indira Gandhi government in pursuit of a socialistic pattern of society. Its goal was "bringing about an equitable distribution of land in urban agglomerations to subserve the common good."[217]

In practical terms, the government wanted to curb the increase in land prices and promote low-income housing through socialisation of urban land. For example, the prices had increased 100 percent in Delhi and other big cities between 1970 and 1975.[218] A study by Ballabh Prasad Acharya, titled "The Indian Urban Land Ceiling Act, A Critique of the 1976 Legislation, Policy of Land Acquisition and Development: Analysis of an Indian Experience," under the McNamara Fellowship Program of the World Bank, stated: "The shortage of urban land, speculative land prices, disturbing trends in the urban land market, the equity considerations and the failure of previous legal measures suggested the necessity of much more stronger action by the government."[219]

The preamble of the Act describes it as

> an Act to provide for the imposition of a ceiling on vacant land in urban agglomerations, for the acquisition of such land in excess of the ceiling limit, to regulate the construction of buildings on such lands and for matters connected therewith, with a view to preventing the concentration of urban land in the hands of few persons and speculation and profitability therein and with a view to bringing about an equitable distribution of land in urban agglomeration to subserve the common good.[220]

However, the debate over the usefulness of this Act in meeting its objectives continues in academic circles decades after its repeal in most Indian states.

Most analyses say the Act failed to make a difference to the availability of land in urban India. In fact, there is evidence to show that the law, far from increasing the availability of land, actually constrained its supply, and, thus, served to increase land prices. Then, applications for exemptions from the implementation of its stringent provisions and the process of granting such permissions emerged as a major source of corruption, and this became yet another avenue for rent seeking by the concerned petty officials and mid- and senior-level bureaucrats.

The Act mandated the government to acquire vacant land in excess of the ceiling limit and make it available to the public at large at reasonable prices, subject to certain exemptions. In practice, the government could acquire only a limited quantum of land. According to the Annual Report of the Ministry of Works and Housing for 1980–81, state governments acquired only 1,925 ha of vacant land as follows:[221]

	State	**Area in ha**
1.	Andhra Pradesh	94.19
2.	Bihar	0.21
3.	Gujarat	64.27
4.	Karnataka	185.52
5.	Madhya Pradesh	182.52
6.	Maharashtra	1,103.00
7.	Rajasthan	10.44
8.	Uttar Pradesh	240.79
9.	West Bengal	44.66

Huge parcels of land were granted exemptions from the Act. The 1,925 ha acquired under the Act was insignificant compared to the 40,393 ha (38,599 ha + 1,794 ha) granted exemption.[222]

The study by Acharya referred to above concludes that

> despite the great promises and rosy pictures offered by the Urban Land (Ceiling and Regulation) Act, 1976, it is unfortunately true that the Act has not only been a failure in the sense that the objectives set by its founding fathers could not be achieved but also (and much worse) that the results have been just the opposite of what was expected. In short, the Act has so far not lived up to its expectations.[223]

- **Subsidising rail passenger fares by raising freight rates:**

  Remember the time when India had a separate Railway Budget? And remember the criteria most people used to judge whether it was a "good" budget or a "bad" one? I remember many of my relatives declaring the rail budget good if passenger fares were left untouched. Never mind if freight rates were increased to subsidise any losses the railways suffered as a result of offering passenger fares at less than cost.

  The logic appeared unimpeachable: Individuals paid for tickets; they deserved to be protected. Companies paid for freight; they could afford to pay extra for transporting their goods from Place A to Place B. Therefore, it was justified to protect individual budgets and pass on the burden of revenue hikes to companies.

  This was the logic sold to the people by India's socialist leaders, and a vast majority of people accepted this at face value without questioning it. But what the leaders did not tell the people—and what my relatives and others like them did not realise—was that ultimately, it was common people like them who were picking up the tab for the higher freight rates in the form of higher prices of all the things they were buying.

  As a result of the steady increase in freight rates over several decades, Indian logistics costs as a percentage of GDP were among the highest in the world. Although logistics costs have been brought down in recent years, they are still higher than those in India's peer nations. This is one of the major contributors to the high cost of production in India and one of the main causes of the country's lack of competitiveness vis-à-vis Vietnam and other ASEAN nations.

- **High tax rates:**

The Indian government has traditionally taxed incomes as well as goods and services at high rates and often imposed multiple taxes on the same products. High income taxes were justified in the name of ushering in a socialistic pattern of society. In 1974–75, the then Finance Minister Y.B. Chavan "reduced" income tax rates to 70 percent for incomes above Rs 70,000 per annum from a jaw-dropping level of 97.5 percent, which had been imposed a few years earlier. Along with a surcharge of 10 percent, the actual marginal tax rate was still an exceptionally extortionist 77 percent.

Given such high levels of taxation, the minuscule size of the tax-paying middle class and the severe restrictions on legal avenues of earning money, it was not surprising that the savings rate was poor, ranging from under 10 percent in 1951 to just over 23 percent in 1991. It was about 9.5 percent when Nehru passed away in 1964 and about 15 percent when Indira Gandhi was assassinated in 1984.[224] Therefore, the investment rate also remained low through these years and the economy continued to struggle.

Another consequence of high taxes was rampant evasion and the proliferation of black money. High rates of customs duties on a host of foreign goods encouraged a thriving market for smuggled goods, as Bollywood captured so vividly in the 1970s and 1980s. The incidence of smuggling gold and consumer goods reduced significantly once duties and taxes were cut in the mid-1980s.

- **Treating tourism as a luxury:**
  The socialist state treated tourism as a luxury and taxed it at high rates. It also did little to encourage domestic tourism on a massive scale. As a result, India lags behind in the global tourism map.

  All over the world, tourism is a major employment generator and provides jobs not only to people who directly work in hotels and the logistics industries, but also helps the local economies of the tourist destinations by generating additional business for restaurants, snack bars, curio shops, memento shops, photography studios (in a bygone era), horse owners, street food vendors, etc.

  It also creates opportunities at every step of the economic ladder and provides livelihoods to people from all strata of society. It also generates large revenues for the local, state and central governments.

  By neglecting this and mis-labelling tourism as a luxury pursuit of the rich, the government missed a major opportunity to generate employment and earn revenues.

No Country Is Too Small for Comparison

Many people argue that Singapore is not worth the

comparison, as it is so small, a mere dot on the map of the world. The argument against that is that being small does not guarantee success. As discussed in the foregoing passages, Singapore succeeded because Lee Kuan Yew managed to overcome the multifaceted challenges that the country faced in the years following its independence and exit from the Malaysian Federation.

South Korea, Taiwan and Hong Kong also faced unique and seemingly insurmountable challenges. Instead of caving in or becoming prisoners of the prevailing ideological orthodoxy of the 1950s–1970s, the leaders of these countries learned their development mantras by trial and error, shedding ideas that did not deliver results and continuing with programmes that showed promise. In addition, all of them invested in their people and spent large sums of money in educating them.

It is only with great effort, vision, perseverance and an open mind that the leaders of these countries managed to take their countries from being hopeless Third World basket cases to the ranks of the developed First World nations in the span of half a century.

If India is now playing catch up with countries that once looked to it for leadership, the responsibility must lie at the doors of the leaders who led us in those crucial decades when our peers were pushing ahead.

9

Nehru and Indira Seriously Undermined Democracy

Republican states gave birth to the world's first democracies in ancient Vaishali in modern-day Bihar. In more recent centuries, though, India had been ruled by a succession of absolute monarchs whose realms ranged from a few square miles in distant corners of the country to vast empires stretching from Kashmir in the north to the seas in the south, from the borders of Assam in the east to Kandahar in Afghanistan in the west.

In the last 190 years before Independence, she had been ruled for 100 years by history's most powerful multinational corporation, the British East India Company, and the last 90 years by a viceroy representing the British monarch. In the last couple of decades of British rule, the colonial masters had given Indians a limited taste of democracy by allowing some civic bodies and, from 1935 onwards, the provinces to be ruled by elected Indians with limited political authority. But, at the grassroots level, India's 6,50,000-plus villages continued with their millennia-old democratic practice of electing their headmen.

So, it was not entirely true that the Indian public was suddenly exposed to democracy and universal adult franchise when the British departed. However, democracy in Independent India was undermined from the very beginning by the charisma of tall leaders who rode their strong personal connect with voters to push agendas and programmes often at variance with the promises that had got them elected. Jawaharlal Nehru and Indira Gandhi, in particular, used their personal charisma to continue pushing their agendas long after it became clear that these policies were leading India to economic oblivion.

To Nehru's credit—and for this every Indian must remain grateful to him—it must be said that he did not become the absolute dictator that many of his contemporary anti-colonial heroes in other newly independent countries evolved into. It is also equally true that he was not quite the unalloyed exemplar of democratic rectitude that his followers have claimed him to be.

Historian and Nehru biographer Ramachandra Guha did recognise that Nehru had become "arrogant." He told EducationWorld:

> ...when Patel died in 1950, and C. Rajagopalachari left the Union Cabinet to become the chief minister of Madras, Nehru didn't have equals with him in government and he became somewhat distant and arrogant and began to see himself as indispensable. Moreover, he stayed on too long in office. After ten years as Prime Minister, he should have retired.[225]

Guha, who is, without doubt, one of India's finest and most respected intellectuals, however, chose to overlook the many instances of Nehru's non-democratic behaviour when he wrote in his 2002 article:

> First, Nehru was without question the chief architect of our democracy. It was he, more than any other nationalist,

> who promoted universal franchise and the multi-party system. He respected other Congressmen and Opposition leaders, and honoured the freedom of press and independence of the judiciary.[226]

Whether India's first Prime Minister deserved such an encomium is debatable. As we have seen in Chapter 1, Nehru found it difficult to pull along with then Congress President Purushottam Das Tandon, who had been Sardar Patel's nominee for the post shortly after Independence. Following the Sardar's death in 1950, the relationship between the Prime Minister and the party president went downhill, making Tandon's position untenable. He resigned.

Instead of risking another independent-minded president who might not acknowledge his primacy and to preclude the possibility of the emergence of an alternative centre of power, Nehru, who was undoubtedly the most popular Congress leader then, got himself elected as the party president. By occupying the two most powerful positions in the government and the party, Nehru ensured that there would be no institutional opposition to his agenda. This diluted the principle of separation of powers and weakened the foundations of democracy early in the life of the young republic.

A few years prior to this, Nehru had another crucial face-off with another Congress president, which critically weakened inner party democracy. By temperament, party affairs did not interest Nehru much; his disinclination to involve the party in the governance of the country came bubbling forth when he became Prime Minister and, thus, had no further use for the party except as an instrument to fight elections. Acharya J.B. Kripalani was Congress president at the time of Independence. The government did not think it fit to consult him or engage with him in any meaningful manner in the framing of official policies. When his protests fell on deaf ears, he resigned.

In his book *Genesis and Growth of Nehruism*, Sita Ram Goel wrote:

> He has proved himself to be easily the most astute politician among a legion of leaders left to this country during thirty long years of Mahatma Gandhi's stewardship. He has tamed or beaten or driven into wilderness not only the so-called "mature and hard-headed" men of the Congress Right but also the "fire-eating rabble-rousers" of the Congress Left… The other Congress leaders may still continue to intrigue against each other… but all of them put together are too weak and demoralized to challenge his authority.[227]

Sidelining everyone who disagreed with him and his inability to get along with such leaders were definitely not a sign of respect towards his colleagues and opposition leaders. This aspect of his politics and leadership mantra has been carefully airbrushed out of popular history, in order to portray him as a true democrat.

First Amendment: Curbed Free Speech, Curtailed Judicial Powers

Nehru's ambivalent attitude towards democracy was also on display in his decision to pass the First Amendment of the Indian Constitution. This amendment had two controversial aspects: the first was placing reasonable restrictions on the fundamental right guaranteeing freedom of speech; the other was the provision to put certain laws beyond the scope of judicial review by placing them in the Ninth Schedule of the Constitution.

Bharatiya Jan Sangh founder Shyama Prasad Mookerjee led the opposition to the First Amendment inside and outside Parliament and called it "scandalous." Nehru, as was his wont and in a strategy that was to become his signature, turned to rhetoric instead of countering Mookerjee on merit. Calling him a liar, Nehru stood his ground and carried the day on the strength of his political capital. Completely belying later claims that he stood resolutely on the side of press freedom, he accused the free press of "poisoning the minds of the younger generation, degrading their mental integrity and moral standards."[228]

It defies logic as to how this could be interpreted as a defence of free speech, press freedom, and democracy. But history does not necessarily remember facts. It usually remembers what historians and biographers record. On this count, Independent India's early rulers were fortunate...

The Ninth Schedule is a kind of shield to protect some laws from judicial review. It was inserted into the Indian Constitution with the passage of Article 31B by the Nehru government in 1951 to protect laws on land reforms, in response to a Supreme Court decision that laws enacted by Parliament could be challenged if they violated the fundamental rights guaranteed by the Constitution.

This constitutional safehouse was inserted in the statute books to ensure that legislation on land reforms and *zamindari* abolition could not be struck down by the courts on the grounds that they were in contravention of the provisions relating to the then Fundamental Right to Property. However, over the decades, about 250-odd legislations have found their way into this schedule.

While the goal of protecting *zamindari* abolition laws was commendable, the existence of the schedule provides governments the option of protecting even patently unconstitutional laws from judicial scrutiny. This is inherently anti-democratic and Nehru, as the author of this provision, must bear responsibility for its consequences. How this serves democracy can also be debated.

Bans on Books and Films Betray Intolerance of Contrarian Viewpoints

In this era of short memory spans and high decibel propaganda wars, an impression has gained ground that the culture of bans in India began with the Rajiv Gandhi government's decision to ban Salman Rushdie's *Satanic Verses* in 1988. Popular, politically unaffiliated opinion has come to believe that the preceding Indira Gandhi era was an aberration and that Nehru's long reign was the golden age of liberal values, marked by freedom of thought and expression.

But if one keeps the rhetoric, hero worship and political one-upmanship aside and goes purely by facts, it will become evident that Nehru's track record on liberalism is a lot more mixed.

In a post on May 1, 2023, on X, scientist, author and public intellectual Anand Ranganathan listed sixteen books banned by the Nehru government. These include Stanley Wolpert's *Nine Hours to Rama*, Nasiri's *Chandra Mohini*,

Menen's *The Ramayana*, Godse's *My Testimony*, and Lawrence's *Lady Chatterley's Lover*, among others. That is not all. His liberal, left-of-centre, socialist government also banned films like Mrinal Sen's *Neel Akasher Neeche* and *Gokul Shankar*.

Nehru's record as a defender of democratic values gets more chequered when one considers that actor Balraj Sahni was arrested in 1949 for participating in a protest by striking mill workers. And lyricist Majrooh Sultanpuri was jailed for a full year in 1951 for criticising Nehru's decision to join the Commonwealth and for comparing him with German dictator Adolf Hitler.

Nehru was a qualified barrister though he never seriously practiced law for a living. If he had, and in case he was given a brief to defend his own track record as a liberal and a democrat, he would have had to admit that he had been given a weak brief and that there was a mountain of irrefutable evidence against him.

Nehru's conduct would fail the test of the statement wrongly attributed to Voltaire but actually penned by his biographer: "I disagree with what you say, but I will defend to the death your right to say it." Whether or not the French philosopher actually uttered these words is immaterial. They have, over time, come to define a classical liberal. Even Nehru's most ardent fan will be hard put to place his track record within the confines of that definition.

All in the Family

In an unprecedented development that chipped away further at the scaffolding of Indian democracy, Indira Gandhi was elected Congress president in 1959. The government and the party were in the firm grip of one family. And two members of the same family held the two most powerful positions in the country for the first time in history.

This was clearly against all democratic norms and made for very poor optics, especially in the light of Nehru's high-sounding rhetoric on democratic norms and liberal values.

Soaring Rhetoric Becomes a Substitute for Delivery

Any programme to pull an underdeveloped country out of its backwardness requires an all-hands-on-deck approach and a leader with both the vision to chart out where he wants to take his nation as well as the ability to get into the nitty-gritty of political management to ensure that all programmes remain on track to deliver the results they were designed for. But Nehru was too much of an aristocratic patriarch. Once he decided that science and technology could solve India's problems, he focused his attention on a few headline-grabbing initiatives like IITs, space research, atomic research, etc., completely neglecting the more mundane issues that affected the day-to-day lives of ordinary Indians. These initiatives were important and have paid India handsome dividends, but, in the final analysis, impacted only a tiny sliver of the country's population.

A few years into his Prime Ministership, Nehru began to get distanced from the reality of India's myriad problems as he interacted mainly with the high priests of science and administration, inaugurating scientific institutions and delivering visionary lectures at high profile conferences. The *Times of India* did not mince words in saying that Nehru remained "in the clouds."[229] Science "freed him of politically difficult redistribution conflicts and the administratively cumbersome apparatus of a modern welfare state," Ashoka Mody wrote in his book *India Is Broken*.[230]

Sympathy for Absolute Dictatorships

In his book *Glimpses of World History*, Nehru stated:

> I have not included the Soviet Union in the above list of dictatorships, because the dictatorship there, although as ruthless as any other, is of a different type. It is not the dictatorship of an individual or a small group, but of a well-organized political party basing itself on the workers. They call it the "dictatorship of the proletariat."...
>
> I have referred to democracy as "formal" in the preceding paragraph. The communists say that it was not real democracy; it was only a democratic shell to hide the fact that one class ruled over the others. According to them, democracy covered the dictatorship of the capitalist class. It was plutocracy, government by the wealthy. The much-paraded vote given to the masses gave them only the choice of saying once, in four or five years, whether a certain person, X, might rule over them and exploit them or another person, Y, should do so. In either event the masses were to be exploited by the ruling class. Real democracy can only come when this class rule and exploitation end and only one class exists. To bring about this socialist state, however, a period of the dictatorship of the proletariat is necessary so as to keep down all capitalist and bourgeois elements in the population and prevent them from intriguing against the workers' state. In Russia this dictatorship is exercised by the Soviets in which all the workers and peasants and other "active" elements are represented. Thus, it becomes a dictatorship of the 90 per cent, or even 95 per cent, over the remaining 10 or 5 per

> cent. That is the theory. In practice the Communist Party controls the Soviets, and the ruling clique of communists control the Party. And the dictatorship is as strict, so far as censorship and freedom of thought or action are concerned, as any other. But as it is based on the good will of the workers it must carry the workers with it. And, finally, there is no exploitation of the workers or any other class for the benefit of another. There is no exploiting class left. If there is any exploitation, it is done by the State for the benefit of all. Russia, it is worth remembering, never had the democratic form of government. It jumped in 1917 from autocracy to communism.[231]

This passage does showcase Nehru's soft corner for the "dictatorship of the proletariat" that is apparently, in his estimation, bereft of exploitation as "there is no exploiting class left."

So how does this admiration for Soviet totalitarianism square with his image as a liberal democrat whose heart beat for the people? And what exactly did he mean by "Russia, it is worth remembering, never had the democratic form of government. It jumped in 1917 from autocracy to communism." It will be fair to suggest that this passage does indicate a disdain for democracy, which is borne out by many of his acts of omission and commission as Prime Minister.

A Fair Self-Appraisal

In 1937, an article titled "*The Rashtrapati*" appeared in *The Modern Review* of Calcutta. Written under the pen name Chanakya, it said:

> He [Nehru] has all the makings of a dictator in him—vast popularity, a strong will directed to a well-defined purpose,

> energy, pride, organizational capacity, ability, hardness, and, with all his love of the crowd, an intolerance of others and a certain contempt for the weak and the inefficient... in this revolutionary epoch, Caesarism is always at the door, and is it not possible that Jawaharlal might fancy himself as a Caesar? Therein lies danger for Jawaharlal and for India. For it not through Caesarism that India will attain freedom, and though she may prosper a little under a benevolent and efficient despotism, she will remain stunted and the day of the emancipation of her people will be delayed.
>
> ...men like Jawaharlal, with all their capacity for great and good work, are unsafe in democracy. A little twist and Jawaharlal might turn a dictator sweeping aside the paraphernalia of a slow-moving democracy. He might still use the language and slogans of democracy and socialism, but we all know how fascism has fattened on this language and cast it away as useless lumber.[232]

The article sent tremors through both the higher echelons of the Congress and its rank and file, as Nehru was then the Congress President. These tremors gave way to consternation when it emerged later that the author of the article was none other than Nehru himself.

Throughout his life, Nehru had displayed a disarming ability to judge himself and his actions correctly, though he did not always act to correct the flaws he so correctly identified. His frank admission on the failure of planning to ameliorate the lot of millions of Indians and his regret at not being able to reform the Indian bureaucracy stand out as shining examples of unbiased self-assessment.

Yes, Nehru did not become a dictator and a fascist his many detractors claim he did, but the series of small steps that weakened the foundations of the fledgling Westminster model of democracy in India paved the way for his daughter to become the absolute ruler her father feared he might become.

Nehru died on May 27, 1964. Despite the rhetoric, the propaganda, and the Plans, Indians were not too much more educated, wealthier, or better off than they had been 17 years previously, when Nehru unfurled the tricolour at the Red Fort for the first time.

Erudite, popular, and well-loved till the end, Nehru left behind a thousand unfulfilled ambitions and broken dreams—and about 490 million people unsure about what tomorrow held for them. Experts and analysts feared for the country's future. Like India, Brazil had also tried to follow the heavy industries route to development and failed—and this had pushed it back into a dictatorship. Would India follow suit? Dark days seemed to lie ahead.

But, despite his obvious failures, it must be said in Nehru's defence that when he started out in 1947, there was no template for him to follow—not even the failures of other leaders he could have learned from. Never before had any country awoken from 1,000 years of servitude and set out to modernise itself with nothing but hope and the good wishes of a sixth of humanity. Stabilising the partition-ravaged nation and giving it a sense of purpose, even if not in full measure, will go down as his greatest contribution to India.

Indira Gandhi Crosses the Line

More than two centuries ago, the fourth US President James Madison had warned about the risk of democracy getting derailed from within. "Men of fractious tempers, of local prejudices, or of sinister design, may by intrigue, by corruption, or by other means, first obtain the suffrages, and then betray the interests of the people."[233]

Ironically, it was not a man but a frail woman, Indira Gandhi, reputed to be the only man in her Cabinet, who hijacked India's democracy while occupying the office of Prime Minister of the country by inflicting "intense damage" on "democratic norms. For when norms break, democracy goes into a 'death spiral.'"[234]

According to Ashoka Mody, norms are people's beliefs in the right things to do. "When those norms are anchored in a personal morality, they become a social asset because they foster the trust for well-functioning markets and political institutions." When these norms break down, people feel they are free to stray from the straight and narrow path if it results in personal gain. He noted:

> Democratic cooperative action with long horizons become impossible. Education and health infrastructure suffer, cities fall into disrepair, abuse of environment goes unchecked, and justice is no longer blind. Moral norms and trust are easy to destroy because any breach makes it uncertain they will work again. Following Mrs Gandhi's example, cheating in economic and social life became habitual because as more people began to cheat, everyone felt the need to cheat.[235]

This had a domino effect and resulted in a further fraying of democratic norms. The balance of powers between the three arms of the government got diluted as the executive gained primacy over the judiciary and Parliament. Result: Indian democracy found itself on a steep and slippery slope.

Missed Opportunity

Even as Indira Gandhi's rule led to a progressive moral decay in the country's public life, she did little to improve the economy. Throughout her 16 years in power in two stints, she did not once articulate or present a coherent economic programme for the regeneration of the country. Instead, she depended on shrill, populist and socialist rhetoric that she made no effort to implement. In retrospect, it is clear that these were designed to woo the common Indian with only rosy but hollow promises.

She operated on the basis of slogans. This was the period when countries in East and South East Asia began to forge ahead. At the beginning of her second stint in power, China began its dramatic climb up the global economic ladder. If only she had leveraged the massive support she enjoyed to pivot the country towards growth, instead of expending all her energies on assuming dictatorial powers, she could have completely changed India's development trajectory. Instead, her rule will go down in history as a big missed opportunity.

But before Indira Gandhi began to undermine democracy from within, she took great pains to cement her connect with the electorate. She jumped into the 1967 electoral campaign with great gusto. According to Katherine Frank, she "covered 15,000 miles" and addressed hundreds of public meetings. "All over the country, she drew enormous crowds—larger even than those who had come to see Nehru." She was deeply aware of her aristocratic heritage and milked the sentimental attachment that the people had with the Nehru legacy. But

> her approach and her language were populist; she spoke in the regional language; she wore her sari as the local women did and ate their food with her fingers. But at the same time, Indira appeared lofty and awesome, copiously garlanded, immaculate in a sea of whirling dust as her Prime Ministerial car roared to a halt before a huge crowd. It was an unbeatable combination.[236]

Environmental Damage Caused Social Injustice

Environmental challenges kept mounting by the 1980s. Heavy irrigation was resulting in widespread soil salinity and waterlogging. Indiscriminate digging of wells was depleting the levels of groundwater. The poor found their shallow wells going dry, coliform organisms (pathogens related to human faeces) in River Yamuna jumped to 24 million in every 100 ml of water in Delhi, compared to only 7,500 before it entered the city.[237] Pollution levels were beginning to rise alarmingly as a result of thermal power plants and the rising vehicular traffic in cities. These were causing health problems, especially for the poor.

India's economic growth was not only damaging the environment but was severely hurting the poor while benefitting the rich. Indira Gandhi's socialist model of development was, thus, resulting in grave social injustice.

Emergency: The Culmination of a Series of Steps to Undermine Democracy

Indira Gandhi declared Emergency on June 25, 1975. She shed all pretence of being democratic, assumed the powers of a dictator, suspended fundamental rights and jailed the entire opposition and thousands of activists around the country.

All the while, she continued her tirade against the alleged shortcomings of democracy. In a shocking statement unbecoming of a Prime Minister who had won two popular mandates, she said: "In India, democracy has given too much licence to the people."[238] This showed in no uncertain terms her utter disdain for the people who had placed their trust in her.

Harsh and heavy-handed censorship of every publication in the country ensured that such statements did not gain wide currency, and enabled her to clamp down on all criticism. And jailing all Opposition leaders ensured that the public anger and widespread discontent her decision generated could be contained to an extent for the time being. Doordarshan and All India Radio were tightly controlled by the government; they disseminated only what the government wanted the people to see and hear. And the few foreign publications allowed into the country were censored before being circulated in India. And foreign travel was beyond the reach of all but the richest Indians. So, the government found it relatively easy to clamp down on news it did not want people to know.

Questioned about the curbs all around, an unnamed official told *New York Times* correspondent J. Anthony Lukas, during the Emergency:

> It is only reporters like yourself and your counterparts among India's middle class who worry about such things as freedom of expression. What most of our people care about is filling their bellies. We are tired of being a workshop of failed democracy. The time has come to exchange some of our vaunted individual rights for some economic development.[239]

Long years of disdain for democracy at the top of the political food chain was rubbing off on those at lower levels and was bursting forth in the attitudes of officials who served the government in senior positions. Given this arrogant and dismissive view on their countrymen, is it any surprise that no one in a position of authority was bothered that the thousands of crores being spent on welfare and development were not reaching their intended beneficiaries?

Nehruvian policies, which had made the rich richer and the poor poorer, had brought India to a new and unexpected crossroads—it was now both a dictatorship and a plutocracy. It had two clear classes: a tiny sliver of mostly English-educated elite had emerged as the new ruling class; and the vast mass of Indians had willy-nilly become the ruled.

The British rulers, whom the earlier generations had spent decades fighting, had been replaced by a new elite comprising the Brown Sahibs and their compradors. There was little change in the lot of the ruled.

10

The Report Card: India Just About Scraped Through with a Third Division

How should one rate India's performance in the first 44 years of its journey as an independent nation? And why 44 years? On what parameters should we judge her performance?

In this analysis of India's performance between 1947 and 1991, the economy has been given prime space. Factors that impact economic growth, such as policies, politics, bureaucracy, education, infrastructure, corruption and the like, have been discussed in detail, and comparisons have been made with other developing countries in Asia.

The first 44 years have been considered because it was during this period that India followed a particularly restrictive, state-led development model that stifled private enterprise and put in place a complex web of bureaucratic controls to regulate almost every aspect of economic activity. For want of a better term to describe it, it has been labelled Nehruvianism or Nehruvian socialism, after the man who set the tone for the policies that defined that period. Facing imminent bankruptcy, India changed course at the end of that period and chose a market-led model of development that has served it well since then.

The year 1991 can, thus, be considered a major inflexion point—the epiphany moment—in India's journey towards developed country status.

Interestingly, for a strongly democratic polity, the first 44 years of Independence were dominated by one political family—the Nehru–Gandhis. Jawaharlal Nehru ruled for 17 years, his daughter Indira Gandhi for 16 years, and her son Rajiv Gandhi for 5 years. Thus, the family ruled for 38 of the first 44 years. India saw as many as five Prime Ministers—Lal Bahadur Shastri, Morarji Desai, Charan Singh, V.P. Singh, and Chandrasekhar—in the remaining six years. Every single Prime Minister during this period was either a Congressman or an ex-Congressman, and all of them largely believed in the same set of political and economic values that were enunciated, initiated and implemented by the first Prime Minister.

So, any attempt to judge India's performance during this period effectively becomes a judgment and a report card on the philosophy of Nehru and the track record of his family.

The Remit of This Report Card

India was among the first Asian countries to set out on the path of economic development in 1947. Other countries—most notably South Korea, Singapore, Taiwan, Hong Kong, Malaysia, Thailand, Indonesia, the Philippines, and China—followed suit in the next few decades.

By 1991, all of them had reasonably long runs as independent nations, following policies each country considered appropriate for its stage of development. Let us take the analogy of a class where India had studied since

1947. Others joined the class later—mid-term. If they were all to pass out in 1991, how would India's performance be rated?

Going by the fulsome praise heaped on Nehru by his followers as the "Builder of Modern India," it would appear as if he had topped the class and passed with First Division and a Distinction. Given the adulation surrounding Indira Gandhi, her performance would not be rated too far behind her father's. Rajiv Gandhi did not rule long enough, but he did leave an impact by kicking off India's technology revolution—in the information and technology and telecom sectors. For this, many of the experts, who give his grandfather and mother such high marks, also place him in the same performance bracket.

The Reality Check

These rosy ratings are justified by citing various points of evidence, all cherry picked to show each leader and his/her achievements in the best possible light—these include the birth of several heavy industries, the setting up of the IITs and IIMs, the setting up of Indian Space Research Organisation (ISRO) and Bhabha Atomic Research Centre (BARC), the victory in the war of 1971, the so-called "peaceful atomic tests" of 1974, the transformation of a food-deficit country into a net exporter of food grains following the success of the Green Revolution, and a similar transformation of India's milk economy after the White Revolution following the success of Amul.

But, however much one tries to burnish a student's performance to make it look better than it is—with these cherry-picked examples, which were the few honourable exceptions rather than the rule—a sea of red ink on the report card gives the game away. All the spin about how Nehru, Indira Gandhi and Rajiv Gandhi built a modern, strong and resilient India cannot disguise the fact that the country was teetering on the brink of bankruptcy by the end of their direct rule. The internationally-lauded success of the IITs and IIMs cannot compensate for the largest population of illiterate people in the world and the abominable state of primary education in India, which are the direct consequence of the lack of vision of Nehru and his successors.

No amount of propaganda can whitewash the fact that the heavy industries that Nehru was so proud of failed spectacularly to solve India's unemployment problem, which kept growing with every passing year between 1951 (the year the First Five Year Plan was launched) and 1991 (the end of the period under review).

One does not have to be an economist; even a person with average intelligence and foresight will know that opting for a capital-intensive development strategy in a country starved of capital and teeming with surplus labour would be a recipe for disaster. Even when it became apparent by the late 1950s that India was driving headlong into a disaster, he made no effort to course correct.

The public sector it engendered was a drag on the economy and a bottomless pit eating up public resources that could have been better deployed in primary education and agriculture. Then, the License Raj, which was a direct result of Nehru's industrial policy gave birth to crony capitalism.

And ISRO and BARC stand as islands of excellence in an ocean of mediocrity and worse.

Nehru's followers claim that he propounded and stood for an Idea of India that was empathetic and inclusive and that he made special efforts to carry the entire nation with him. This philosophy, they add, lies at the root of his vision for India and was carried forward by his daughter and grandson.

Once again, there is little to show for this inclusion beyond the rhetoric. As Nehru himself admitted before his death, the benefits of his planning had not reached millions of needy people. He left behind a country that was starving—and would survive on the largesse of the US government, thanks to its PL480 programme. Then, his failed industrialisation drive left three generations of Indians unemployed and without a hope for a better future, as his dynasty refused to change course even when the examples of other Asian countries showed that alternative means of development were likely to bring better results.

By 1991, all the countries mentioned above were far ahead of India on every count.

This assessment would have been considered blasphemy even two decades ago—punishable with banishment from academia, media and society by the arbiters of public discourse in India.

Then, were Nehru and his successors complete failures? Not quite! Though they were nowhere near the first divisions that many historians and analysts have claimed for them, it would be unfair to say they had flunked the class.

Needed: A Nuanced Review

Their performances merit a more nuanced review.

Yes, Nehruvian socialism did disfigure India's development trajectory beyond recognition and precluded it from achieving its potential for a little more than four decades. Yes, the overwhelming poverty all around, the pervasive corruption, the appalling inefficiency and the abominable state of infrastructure were all the results of the ideological blinkers worn by India's rulers. These make the report card look bad.

On non-economic issues—not part of this book's remit and, therefore, not discussed in the foregoing chapters, but still a critical part of India's successes and failures in the period under review—Nehru blundered by privileging China's interests over India's, when he passed up the opportunity of occupying a seat on the United Nations Security Council on the dubious grounds that China deserved it more. Then, apart from making a complete mess of Kashmir's integration into India, he refused Oman's offer to take over its colony of Gwadar in Pakistan. He declined King Tribhuvan's offer to merge Nepal into India, and also turned down the offer for Coco Islands. He also rejected the offer of the Khan of Kalat (which comprised much of modern-day Balochistan) to accede to India because he (Nehru) wanted a stable and friendly Pakistan—even as India and Pakistan were locked in a confrontation over Kashmir.

These decisions, among many others, highlight Nehru's lack of vision and foresight, as all these now fall under China's sphere of influence. These are classic examples of geo-political self-goals. Yet, they have not received much attention and instead been brushed under the carpet or been airbrushed out of history, in an attempt to make the Nehru years look like some kind of a golden age.

Ironically, India fared worst in precisely those areas which received most of Nehru's personal attention—foreign policy, economy and the country's development trajectory.

Thus, the bright splashes of red in the report card put the few areas marked in blue ink in the shade. But before we explore these areas of good performance, let us digress a little and consider a paper titled "Institutions" in the *Journal of Economic Perspectives* by economist and Nobel laureate Douglass C. North.[240] This paper, which placed institutions at the front and centre of the economic development process, defined institutions as "humanly devised constraints that structure political, economic and social interaction."[241] For example, the failures of many African and South American nations can be traced directly to the shortcomings in their weak institutions, which could not cope with the dynamics of the initiatives implemented in their countries. India, which has much stronger institutions, therefore, managed to withstand the deleterious effects of a succession of bad policies since 1947.

Institutions include a wide range of tangible and intangible values and attributes such as democracy, rule of law, free speech, transparency, accountability, minority rights, inclusiveness, enforcement of rules and regulations, and respect for property rights. It also includes institutions that deal with the environment, education, public order and justice, as well as processes to resolve conflicts and create frameworks that meet both market and non-market needs.

It is the failure of their institutions that prevented many countries in Africa and South America from achieving their potential as internal conflicts dragged down their economies. In India, on the other hand, it was the strength of its institutions that enabled it to weather the crises arising from caste tensions, religious polarisation, regional disparities, democratic erosion, and serious attempts by the political executive to capture those very institutions and create a "committed bureaucracy" and a "committed judiciary."

In India, Nehru's supporters can rightly claim that he was the key architect of these institutions, which have stood the test of time. They weathered occasional efforts by Nehru himself to find ways around them, survived the storm of the Emergency and withstood the strain imposed by a series of disastrous policy choices. They also survived—wounded and scarred but still fundamentally unchanged—efforts by Nehru's successors to weaken them and hollow them out from within.

Therefore, instead of looking only at results and marking his report card accordingly, if we look at processes, Nehru's record will look a lot better. It might still not measure up to the achievements of India's peer nations, but it will definitely balance out some of the red ink that we spoke of above. Already, Nehru, the builder of institutions, is looking a lot more successful than Nehru, the socialist Stalin admirer.

As discussed in Chapter 9, many anti-colonial heroes who were elected to head their countries after independence from their colonial masters became dictators of single party governments. Nehru resisted the urge. Although he placed reasonable restrictions on free speech, jailed Majrooh

Sultanpuri, and banned several books and movies, he never went all the way and clamped down on free speech. Although he did amend the Constitution to create the Ninth Schedule, he did not openly interfere with the judiciary. Though he misused Article 356 to dismiss the democratically elected communist government of Kerala in 1959, he extended constitutional courtesies to other chief ministers.

So, despite some horrendous missteps and some ill-conceived interventions, he did allow the various institutions of the state and society sufficient space to grow and plant their roots in the India. This allowed the country to develop a political culture in tune with its lived values of inclusivity, conciliation, tolerance and acceptance.

These are no mean feats and his report card, in all fairness, must include these as well. Taken together, the sum of the positives and the negatives will leave, at the end of the exercise, a small sum on the positive side of his balance sheet, in my opinion.

A highly respected columnist had in 2022 rated Nehru's performance as undeserving of a First Division but rated it as high Second Division. The propaganda blitz that we had been subjected to in school had led many of us to believe his performance as Prime Minister deserved a First Division with a Distinction. But any performance must be ranked relative to that of others in the same class.

If the most popular pupil in class fails in several subjects, just about passes in some others and secures an aggregate that is just above the minimum pass marks, would you not consider it very brave if the teacher gave him the Student of the Year crown—especially when other lower profile students scored much higher marks than the star did in every subject?

Therefore, Nehru's report card should, in all fairness, reflect that he has just about scraped through with pass marks. A Third Division and definitely nowhere near a Distinction.

Indira's Report Card: Fail

If Nehru has just about passed, how about his daughter Indira, whose track record as Prime Minister is a story of a series of missed opportunities, cynical misuse of authority and rampant corruption?

If Nehru scored well for building institutions and for not interfering too heavily in their workings, history will judge Indira Gandhi harshly for actively interfering in the working of every institution and dealing a near fatal blow to democracy in India in the form of the Emergency.

Not only did she not do anything to prevent the hijacking of institutions, she also actively tried and often succeeded in bending them to her will. Her promotion of her son Sanjay Gandhi as an extra-constitutional authority answerable to no one, her decision to meddle in the appointment of the Chief Justice of India, her government's attempts to create a committed bureaucracy and judiciary, and her brazen destruction of inner party democracy by nominating candidates for every position in the party as well as Congress chief ministers, are directly responsible for badly damaging some institutions and permanently weakening the foundations of democracy and liberalism in the country.

She also turned a blind eye to and encouraged the spread of corruption, the criminalisation of politics and the institutionalisation of crony capitalism as the central mantra of doing business in India. Her rule in two stints is a long laundry list of missed targets, empty rhetoric, damaged institutions and personality cult.

Unlike her father, who left behind a mixed legacy of achievements, failures, and missed opportunities, Indira Gandhi's legacy has few positive features and fewer achievements on the economic and social fronts. But there are still people who cite her nationalisation of banks and coal mines, her decision to abolish privy purses and other princely privileges, and her brave and astute management of the conduct of the campaign to liberate Bangladesh from Pakistani occupation.

But the stellar achievement of the Indian military on the battlefield and her brilliant handling of the foreign policy challenge posed by US support for Islamabad were compromised by the surrender at Shimla, where India let Pakistan off the hook by returning 93,000 prisoners of war (PoWs) without getting anything substantive in return.

As icing on the cake, Pakistani leader Zulfikar Ali Bhutto returned to his country with the sculpture of the priest king, a relic from the Indus–Saraswati Civilisation, which had been in the custody of the National Museum in New Delhi till 1972. The Shimla Agreement created an unwanted world record that is unlikely to be ever beaten—the no-conditions-attached return of PoWs and the gift of the antique statue must be the only instance in the history of warfare of the loser returning home with the spoils of war while the winner only got empty assurances that were forgotten even before the ink had dried on the agreement. Why she signed such an agreement remains one of the big unsolved mysteries of her rule.

Although the government's propaganda machinery played up the Shimla Agreement as a great achievement, the truth could not be hidden for long, and Indira Gandhi must carry the can for not driving home India's advantage and forcing a winner's pact on Pakistan.

Indira Gandhi's policies also fuelled separatism in Punjab and Assam and threatened the unity and integrity of India.

On the positive side, she should be given credit for not getting in the way of the Green Revolution that had been initiated by Lal Bahadur Shastri in his short reign as Prime Minister. She should also get credit for the White Revolution, which transformed India into milk-surplus country. Then, on returning to power in 1980, she shed some of her socialist orthodoxy and marginally loosened the iron fetters on Indian business. This allowed the growth rate to tick upward and helped a small section of hitherto neglected Indians to improve their lot. However, in the absence of widespread reforms, this could not translate into an across-the-board economic boom.

On the basis of this performance, it will not be unfair to say that Indira Gandhi should be given less than pass marks. In other words, she fails, according to this analysis.

Rajiv Gandhi Will Be Remembered by History for Paving the Way for the IT Revolution

The third member of the family to rule India, Rajiv Gandhi, had a tenure of only five years as Prime Minister. Although he soon frittered away the goodwill with which he assumed office and his tenure is now remembered for post-Independence India's most infamous corruption scandal, over kickbacks allegedly paid for the purchase of Bofors howitzers; the political missteps over the Shah Bano judgment; and the shameful manner in which his government oversaw the exit of the then Union Carbide Chairman Warren Anderson from India, out of reach of Indian law for crimes of omission and commission for his company's role in the Bhopal gas tragedy.

Public memory is short, and people tend to remember only dramatic events from the past. So, it has been forgotten that Rajiv Gandhi set in motion two revolutions, the benefits of which India is still reaping. His insistence on technology took India, kicking and screaming, into the computer age. There was widespread opposition to the introduction of computers. Many politicians and almost all the trade unions feared that computerisation would throw millions of workers out of jobs. India should remain eternally grateful that Rajiv Gandhi resisted the immense political pressure to stop the tide of tech and stood his ground. Although he is not given any credit for this decision, at least in public opinion, India's reputation as the world's back office owes a huge debt of gratitude to this one decision. As it often happens in history, this small and unheralded move paved the way for the IT revolution and helped change the course of the Indian economy by giving the country its first world beater.

The other decision that Indians should thank him for is the telecom revolution. By enabling the mushrooming of public telephone booths, he created the atmosphere to change the classification of telephones from luxury good to everyday utility item. The introduction of mobile phones in the following decade was the logical next step.

For these two decisions alone, Rajiv Gandhi should be given a very high score. But he did mess up on various other fronts, thus leaving behind a more mixed legacy. He deserves a high Second Division. In my opinion, he alone among the Prime Ministers from his family will be remembered fondly by history—once the passage of time takes the edge off the partisan carping that currently mars his legacy.

Other PMs, Barring Shastri, Failed to Leave a Mark

The other Prime Ministers ruled for very short tenures—too short to be able to leave any discernible positive impact. But, as mentioned above, Shastri deserves a First Division for having the foresight to initiate the Green Revolution in the face of stiff opposition from several quarters. This one programme changed India's fate and transformed it from an eternally food-deficit country to one that produces enough to feed not only its rising population but also the export markets. He did not live long enough to see his seminal decision pay handsome dividends, but no other Prime Minister in the period under review had a similar positive impact on the lives of so many people. However, he did not rule long enough to have any impact on any other sector.

Morarji Desai will be remembered for driving out Coca-Cola and IBM. For this, he will have to join his *bete noire* Indira Gandhi in the list of failed PMs. Charan Singh, too, did not last long enough to leave any legacy. The same holds true for V.P. Singh and Chandrasekhar.

The biggest indictment of the Nehruvian legacy is that it denied Indians the full benefits of India's hard won political freedom. By keeping Indians in economic chains, successive governments sucked the lifeblood of the economy. By fettering the average Indians' natural dynamism and spirit of innovation, the then governments ensured that India would remain an impoverished Third World country that depended on charity to sustain itself. The stark difference in India's growth and development trajectory after abandoning these policies point to missed opportunity when the global economy was still full of low hanging fruits that India could have harvested to transform itself.

The Overall Score: A Poor Third Division

So, where does this leave India's overall report card, after considering all the eight Prime Ministers who ruled India for the first 44 years of Independence?

Nehru just about passed and touched every aspect of the economy and society. Shastri scored a high First Class but did not impact any sector apart from agriculture. Indira, like her father, touched every facet of public life, but is mainly remembered for weakening every institution she touched. Rajiv Gandhi, the only other full-term Prime Minister, also scored very well, getting a high Second Class. The other Prime Ministers, who ruled for a few months each, have also all failed, according to this analysis.

Summing them all up returns only one verdict: In the first 44 years of Independence, India did not fail, but did not do very well either. Given the evidence at hand, it just about scraped past the pass marks with a Third Division! This becomes all the more clear when one compares India's performance with that of China and its other Asian neighbours in East and South East Asia.

References

1 Ashoka Mody, *India Is Broken*, p. 25

2 Ibid., p. 27

3 Praveen Davar, "The Greatest Indian After the Mahatma: Why Gandhi Chose Nehru to Lead India," *Deccan Chronicle*, November 15, 2018. https://www.deccanchronicle.com/opinion/op-ed/151118/the-greatest-indian-after-the-mahatma-why-gandhi-chose-nehru-to-lead.html

4 Ashoka Mody, *India Is Broken*, p. 28

5 Ibid., p. 28

6 Ibid., p. 29

7 Ibid., p. 31

8 *The Labour Monthly*, Vol. 18, no. 5, May 1936, pp. 282–305 (emphasis added)

9 Swaminathan S Anklesaria Aiyer, "The Caste Basis of Indian Socialism," *The Economic Times*, April 21, 2010. https://economictimes.indiatimes.com/swaminathan-s-a-aiyar/the-caste-basis-of-indian-socialism/articleshow/5838306.cms?from=mdr

10 Ashoka Mody, *India Is Broken*, p. 32

11 "India and the State of Kalat," *Hindustan Times*, August 28, 2006. https://www.hindustantimes.com/india/india-and-the-state-of-kalat/story-AFabUweTII7Av3xEz4eiJO.html

12 The National Archives of the UK. "Fifties Britain." See https://www.nationalarchives.gov.uk/education/resources/fifties-britain/

13 S.S. Gill, *The Dynasty*, p. 94

14 Gurcharan Das, *India Unbound*, p. 94

15 Ibid., p. 94

16 Gurcharan Das, India Unbound, Pp. 175-175

17 Ibid., p. 95

18 Ashoka Mody, *India Is Broken*, p. 62

19 Arvind Panagariya, "Nehru's Real Big Mistake: Heavy Industry Wrongly Got Priority in 1950s. So Even at 75, India Isn't Rich," *The Times of India*, August 19, 2019. https://timesofindia.indiatimes.com/blogs/toi-edit-page/nehrus-real-big-mistake-heavy-industry-wrongly-got-priority-in-1950s-so-even-at-75-india-isnt-rich/

20 Ibid.

21 Ibid.

22 World Bank, 1954, *Current Economic Conditions and Prospects of Brazil*, WH, 23-b, 8 July, Washington DC, ii–iv

23 Ashoka Mody, *India Is Broken*, pp. 66–68

24 "An Erudite Economist," *Financial Express*, January 24, 2003

25 Niranjan Rajadhyaksha, 'The Economics of Jawaharlal Nehru," *Mint*, May 30, 2014

26 Gurcharan Das, *India Unbound*, p. 170

27 Arvind Panagariya, "The Nehru-Era Economic History and Thought," *Moneycontrol*, June 20, 2025. https://www.moneycontrol.com/books/book-extract-the-nehru-era-economic-history-and-thought-by-by-arvind-panagariya-article-13153718.html

28 Ashoka Mody, *India Is Broken*, p. 9

29 Ibid., p. 47

30 Walter Crocker, *Nehru: A Contemporary's Estimate*, pp. 15–16

31 Ibid., p. 41

32 Ibid., p. 42

33 S.S. Gill, *The Dynasty*, p. 80

34 Ashoka Mody, *India Is Broken*, p. 108

35 Ibid., p. 70

36 Ibid.

37 Fundamental Rules, Part I, Chapter I, Extent of Application, FR 2, https://dopt.gov.in/sites/default/files/Compilation_FR_SR_English.pdf

38 Jon S.T. Quah, "Why Singapore Works: Five Secrets of Singapore's Success," *Public Administration and Policy: An Asia-Pacific Journal*, Vol. 21, no. 1, (2018), pp. 5–21

39 Ibid.

40 Ibid.

41 Ibid.

42 See https://liveencounters.net/2019-le-mag/12-december-thinkers-2019/dr-naresh-chandra-saxena-why-is-indian-bureaucracy-not-delivering/

43 Gurcharan Das, *India Unbound*, p. 95

44 S.S. Gill, *The Dynasty*, p. 9

45 Jawaharlal Nehru, *Discovery of India*, p. 50

46 Amit Cowshish, "How the Bureaucracy Has Left the Indian Civil Services Adrift," *The Wire*, March 12, 2021. https://thewire.in/government/bureaucracy-civil-services-india-ias-officers

47 Suman Dubey, "Jawaharlal Nehru: A Troubled Legacy," *India Today*, June 15, 1982. https://www.thenehru.org/2021/06/jawaharlal-nehru-troubled-legacy.html

48 Michael Lipton, *Why Poor People Stay Poor: A Study of Urban Bias in World Development*, p. 13

49 Arun Anand, "Hallmarks of Nehru Model of Government: Corruption, Inefficiency, Nepotism," *Firstpost*, February 12, 2022. https://www.firstpost.com/india/right-word-hallmarks-of-nehru-model-of-governance-corruption-inefficiency-nepotism-10368661.html

50 Tavleen Singh, *Durbar*, p. 73

51 Ibid., p. 96

52 Ibid.

53 S.S. Gill, *The Dynasty*, p. 73

54 S. Gopal, Ravinder Kumar and H.Y. Sharada Prasad, eds., *Selected Works of Jawaharlal Nehru*, Series 2, Vol. 24, p. 34; S.S. Gill, *The Dynasty*, p. 75

55 Puja Mehra, The Hindu, 'Merit-based civil service will boost growth', 21 November, 2014, https://www.thehindu.com/news/national/meritbased-civil-service-will-boost-growth/article6622555.ece

56 Milan Vaishnav and Saksham Khosla, "The Indian Administrative Service Meets Big Data," *Carnegie Endowment for International Peace*, (September 2016), p. 3

57 Krishna Nehru Hutheesing, *Nehru's Letters to His Sister*, p. 187

58 S.S. Gill, *The Dynasty*, p. 74

59 Anjani Mahesh Kumar Cherukuri, Gnaneswhar Pendurthi and Chinmay Rao Chanda, "Dr Subhash Mukhopadhyay (1931–1981): A Pioneer in the Field of Reproductive Medicine," *Cureus*, Vol. 16, no. 9, (September 2024) https://pmc.ncbi.nlm.nih.gov/articles/PMC11452318/#:~:text=On%20October%203%2C%201978%2C%20Dr,Kanupriya%20Agarwal)%2C%20in%20Calcutta.

60 Ibid.

61 Ibid.

62 Ibid.

63 Lancet, https://www.thelancet.com/journals/lancet/article/PIIS0140-6736(05)61584-X/abstract
64 Why the US Pig Heart Transplant Was Different From the 1997 Assam Doc's Surgery, The wire, 13 January, 2022 https://science.thewire.in/health/university-maryland-pig-heart-xenotransplant-dhani-ram-baruah-1997-failed-surgery-arrest/
65 Rahul Karmakar, A pig heart transplant in Assam in 1997, The Hindu, 15 January, 2022, https://www.thehindu.com/sci-tech/science/assam-pioneer-of-pig-heart-transplant-now-working-on-biomolecular-treatment/article38266334.ece
66 https://www.bbc.com/news/health-60681493
67 Jawaharlal Nehru, *The Discovery of India,* p. 221
68 S. Gopal, Ravinder Kumar and H.Y. Sharada Prasad, eds., *Selected Works of Jawaharlal Nehru*, Series 2, Vol. 27, p. 503
69 Milton Friedman, "A Memorandum to the Government of India 1955," November 5, 1955
70 TNN, "India Has a Third of World's Illiterates," *Times of India*, March 8, 2017. https://timesofindia.indiatimes.com/india/india-has-a-third-of-worlds-illiterates/articleshow/916814.cms
71 "Literacy Rate by Country," World Population Review. https://worldpopulationreview.com/country-rankings/literacy-rate-by-country
72 S.S. Gill, *The Dynasty*, pp. 53–54
73 Ashoka Mody, *India Is Broken*, pp. 90–91
74 *Challenge of Education: A Policy Perspective*, Ministry of Education, p. 5. https://cprindia.org/wp-content/uploads/2022/12/Challenge-of-Education-A-Policy-Perspective.pdf
75 Jayakumar Anagol, "Compulsory Primary Education Challenges and Opportunities," CMDR Monograph Series No 22, p. 10

76 Ashoka Mody, *India Is Broken*, pp. 12–13

77 Ibid.

78 Ibid., pp. 44–45

79 Ibid., p. 43

80 Katherine Frank, *Indira: The Life of Indira Nehru Gandhi*, pp. 432–33

81 Ashoka Mody, *India Is Broken*, p. 141

82 S.S. Gill, *The Dynasty*, pp. 58–59

83 *Economic and Political Weekly*, November 21, 1992.

84 See https://righttoeducation.in/sites/default/files/StatusofLearningAchievementsinIndia%5B1%5D.pdf

85 R.K. Karanjia, *The Philosophy of Nehru*, p. 27

86 S.S. Gill, *The Dynasty*, p. 59

87 Maulana Azad, *India Wins Freedom*, Revised Edition, 1988, p. 180

88 Amrit Kaur, "A Friend Without Friends," in *A Study of Nehru*, ed. Rafiq Zakaria, p. 155

89 S.S. Gill, *The Dynasty*, p. 57

90 Macaulay's Minute on Education. February 2, 1835. https://home.iitk.ac.in/~hcverma/Article/Macaulay-Minutes.pdf

91 Rajesh Singh, *Challenges of the India–Bharat Divide: Policies and Perspectives*, Vivekananda International Foundation, January 23, 2018, pp. 4–5

92 Gurcharan Das, *India Unbound*, p. 75

93 Ashoka Mody, *India Is Broken*, pp. 91–92

94 Ibid., p. 93

95 Ibid., pp. 93–95

96 Hemant Singh, "Census 2011: Literacy rate and sex ratio in India since 1901 to 2011," *Jagran Josh*, October 17, 2016. https://www.jagranjosh.com/general-knowledge/census-2011-literacy-rate-and-sex-ratio-in-india-since-1901-to-2011-1476359944-1

97 See https://www.macrotrends.net/global-metrics/countries/CHN/china/literacy-rate

98 Krishna Nehru Hutheesing, *Nehru's Letters to his Sister*, p. 187

99 Briefing Paper, *Seven Lessons from Singapore: What Britain Should Really Learn from the "Singapore Model,"* Social Market Foundation, January 2021, p. 4

100 Ibid.

101 Ashoka Mody, *India Is Broken*, p. 87

102 See https://www.educationworld.in/i-believe-nehrus-greatest-failure-was-to-ignore-primary-education/

103 See https://testbook.com/question-answer/at-independence-about-75-percent-of-indias-p--63f4ddce7cb68076e9748136#:~:text= At%20the%20time%20of%20India's,farming%20or%20related%20agricultural%20activities.

104 Krishna Gupta, "First Five Year Plan: Buttressing Primary Pillars," *Millennium Post*, February 20, 2022. https://www.millenniumpost.in/sundaypost/beacon/first-five-year-plan-buttressing-primary-pillars-468862

105 See https://www.insightsonindia.com/indian-economy-3/agriculture/indian-agriculture-under-the-five-year-plans/

106 S.S. Gill, *The Dynasty*, p. 87; Ashoka Mody, *India is Broken*, p. 67

107 eGyanKosh, Unit 5, "Impact of Land Reforms on Economy." https://egyankosh.ac.in/bitstream/123456789/32696/1/Unit-5.pdf

108 Kwan S. Kim, "The Korean Miracle (1962–1980) Revisited: Myths and Realities in Strategy and Development," Working Paper #166, (Kellog Institute, November 1991)

109 Ibid.

110 Ibid.

111 Ibid.

112 Ashoka Mody, *India Is Broken*, p. 38

113 Ibid., p. 38

114 Michael J. Seth, "An Unpromising Recovery: South Korea's Post-Korean War Economic Development: 1953–1961," *Education About Asia*, Vol. 18, no. 3, (Winter 2013), pp. 42–45

115 Ashoka *Mody, India Is Broken*, p. 39

116 Ashoka Mody, India is broken, P. 40

117 Ibid., p. 41

118 S.S. Gill, *The Dynasty*, p. 67

119 Ibid., p. 65

120 Ibid., p. 68

121 Ashoka Mody, *India Is Broken*, p. 78

122 S.S. Gill, *The Dynasty*, p. 69

123 Ashoka Mody, *India Is Broken*, p. 68

124 See https://www.insightsonindia.com/indian-economy-3/agriculture/indian-agriculture-under-the-five-year-plans/

125 "Collectivization," *Encyclopaedia Britannica.* https://www.britannica.com/money/collectivization

126 Charan Singh, *Joint Farming X-Rayed: The Problem and Its Solution*, p. 123

127 See https://eparlib.nic.in/bitstream/123456789/2966/1/lsd_03_07_17-02-1964.pdf 1162

128 See https://www.macrotrends.net/global-metrics/countries/IND/india/inflation-rate-cpi

129 See https://www.indexmundi.com/AGRICULTURE/?country=in&commodity=wheat&graph=imports

130 Paul Ehlrich, *The Population Bomb*, p. 11

131 Ibid., p. 40

132 Ibid.

133 See https://www.indexmundi.com/agriculture/?country=in&commodity=wheat&graph=imports

134 Gurcharan Das, *India Unbound*, p. 90

135 Nikita Krushchev's keynote address to the Twentieth Congress of the Communist Party of the Soviet Union. February 1956. https://www.marxists.org/archive/khrushchev/1956/02/24.htm

136 Bruce Reidel, *JFK's Forgotten Crisis: Tibet, the CIA, and the Sino-Indian War,* pp. 152–53

137 Kwan S. Kim, "The Korean Miracle (1962–1980) Revisited: Myths and Realities in Strategy and Development," Working Paper #166, (Kellog Institute, November 1991)

138 Ibid.

139 Ibid.

140 World Bank Group, GDP per capita (Current US $)—India. https://data.worldbank.org/indicator/NY.GDP.PCAP.CD?locations=IN

141 "Collectivization," *Encyclopaedia Britannica.* https://www.britannica.com/money/collectivization

142 "Maoism," *Encyclopaedia Britannica.* https://www.britannica.com/topic/Maoism

143 Ashoka Mody, *India Is Broken*, p. 49

144 Ibid., p.99

145 Ibid., p. 200

146 Ibid., pp. 97–98

147 Tavleen Singh, *Durbar*, p. 76

148 S.S. Gill, *The Dynasty*, P. 88

149 Ibid., 89

150 Manjul Paul, The history behind 'Hindu rate of growth', in charts, 9 March, 2023, www.livemint.com, https://www.livemint.com/economy/the-history-behind-hindu-rate-of-growth-in-charts-11678370005198.html

151 Anthony Day, "Transformation of a Man into a Leader of India's Masses," *Los Angeles Times*, October 11, 1996

152 PTI, "Misrepresenting Nehru's Lines from Speech 'Shameful': Priyanka Gandhi Slams PM," *Hindustan Times*, February 6, 2024

153 Gurcharan Das, *India Unbound*, p. 69

154 Vito Tanzi, *Corruption Around the World, Causes, Consequences, Scope, and Cures*, IMF Working Paper, International Monetary Fund, May 1998

155 Ashoka Mody, *India Is Broken*, pp. 106–07

156 Ibid., P. 32

157 Indrajit Hazra, "Hang the Metaphor," *Hindustan Times*, July 23, 2011

158 Ashoka Mody, *India is Broken*, P. 98

159 S.S. Gill, *The Dynasty*, Pp. 144-145

160 Ibid., p. 97

161 Report of the Committee on Prevention of Corruption, Ministry of Home Affairs, Government of India, p. 1

162 Ibid., p. 8

163 Ibid.

164 Ibid., p. 9

165 Ibid.

166 Ashoka Mody, *India Is Broken*, p. 69

167 Ibid., p. 70

168 Ibid.

169 Report of the Committee on Prevention of Corruption, Ministry of Home Affairs, Government of India, pp. 9–10

170 Ibid., p. 10

171 Ibid., p. 12

172 Ibid.

173 Ibid., p. 13

174 Ibid., p. 18

175 Ibid., p. 45

176 Ibid., p. 101

177 Ibid., p. 121

178 Ibid., pp. 53–54

179 Ibid., p. 102

180 Ibid., p. 104

181 Ibid., p. 106

182 "Ray on Ray." https://satyajitray.org/ray-on-ray/

183 Ashoka Mody, *India Is Broken*, p. 196

184 Ibid., p. 197

185 Ibid., p. 198

186 Niranjan Sahoo, *Financing Elections in India: A Scrutiny of Corporate Donation*, ORF, April 9, 2019

187 Kuldip Nayar, *India: The Critical Years*, p. 3

188 Ashoka Mody, *India Is Broken,* p. 148

189 Ibid., p. 155

190 Ibid., p. 192

191 Lee Kew Yuan, *From Third World to First: The Singapore Story—1965–2000*, pp. 3, 9

192 Jon S.T. Quah, "Why Singapore Works: Five Secrets of Singapore's Success," *Public Administration and Policy: An Asia-Pacific Journal*, Vol. 21, no. 1, (2018), pp. 5–21

193 Ibid.

194 Ibid.

195 Ibid.

196 Ibid.

197 Ibid.

198 Akshat Khandelwal, "Nehru's Economic Policy Was Not Wrong—Our Narrative About It Is," *Scroll*, November 14, 2014. https://scroll.in/article/689736/nehrus-economic-policy-was-not-wrong-our-narrative-about-it-is

199 Sanjeev Sabhlok, "What Lee Kuan Yew knew: Lesson to India from Singapore's Transformation: Promote Merit, Devise Incentive Compatible Solutions," *Times of India*, May 17, 2019. https://timesofindia.indiatimes.com/blogs/seeing-the-invisible/what-lee-kuan-yew-knew-lesson-to-india-from-singapores-transformation-promote-merit-devise-incentive-compatible-solutions/

200 World Bank Group, GDP Per Capita, (Current US$)—Singapore

201 World Bank Group, GDP Per Capita, (Current US$)—India

202 Jon S.T. Quah, "Why Singapore Works: Five Secrets of Singapore's Success," *Public Administration and Policy: An Asia-Pacific Journal*, Vol. 21, no. 1, (2018), pp. 5–21

203 Lee Kew Yuan, *From Third World to First: The Singapore Story—1965–2000*, p. 157

204 Aravindam Neelkandam, "Jawaharlal Nehru and How His Love for Marxism Affected India," *Swarajya*, November 14, 2018. https://swarajyamag.com/ideas/jawaharlal-nehru-and-how-his-love-for-marxism-affected-india

205 Sanjeev Sabhlok, "What Lee Kuan Yew knew: Lesson to India from Singapore's Transformation: Promote Merit, Devise Incentive Compatible Solutions," *Times of India*, May 17, 2019. https://timesofindia.indiatimes.com/blogs/seeing-the-invisible/what-lee-kuan-yew-knew-lesson-to-india-from-singapores-transformation-promote-merit-devise-incentive-compatible-solutions/

206 Dipak K. Dash, "Mumbai & Bengaluru Among Most Congested Cities in the World," *Times of India*, February 10, 2022. https://timesofindia.indiatimes.com/india/mumbai-bengaluru-in-top-10-world-cities-on-congestion-parameters/articleshow/89447050.cms

207 Ashoka Mody, *India Is Broken*, pp. 77–78

208 Ibid., p. 78

209 Tavleen Singh, *Durbar*, p. 111

210 Ibid., p. 111

211 Ibid., pp. 111–12

212 Ministry of Power, *Growth of Electricity Sector in India from 1947–2022* (New Delhi: Central Electricity Authority, 2023). https://cea.nic.in/wp-content/uploads/pdm/2023/02/Growth_Book_2022_PDF.pdf

213 https://barrett.dyson.cornell.edu/NEUDC/paper_316.pdf

214 See https://www.marketcalls.in/infographic/tele-density-in-india-infographic.html

215 "Capital Issues Control," The Stock Exchange, Bombay, 1977, p. 1

216 Capital Issues (Control) Act, 1947. https://www.sebi.gov.in/sebi_data/commondocs/may-2019/capitalissue_p.pdf

217 Urban Land Ceiling and Regulation Act, 1976. https://www.mohua.gov.in/upload/uploadfiles/files/ulcra_1976.pdf

218 Lakshmi Srinivas, "Land and Politics in India: Working of Urban Land Ceiling Act, 1976," *Economic and Political Weekly*, Vol. 26, no. 43, (October 26, 1991), pp. 2482–84

219 Ballabh Prasad Acharya, *The Indian Urban Land Ceiling Act: A Critique of the 1976 Legislation Policy of Land Acquisition and Development, Analysis of an Indian Experience,* McNamara Fellowships Program, p. 40

220 Urban Land Ceiling and Regulation Act, 1976

221 Devendra B. Gupta, "Urban Housing in India," World Bank Staff Working Paper, No. 730, (Washington, DC: World Bank, 1985), pp. 148–49

222 Ibid., p. 149

223 Ballabh Prasad Acharya, *The Indian Urban Land Ceiling Act: A Critique of the 1976 Legislation Policy of Land Acquisition and Development, Analysis of an Indian Experience,* McNamara Fellowships Program, p. 49

224 World Bank Group, Gross Domestic Savings (% of GDP)—India

225 See https://www.educationworld.in/i-believe-nehrus-greatest-failure-was-to-ignore-primary-education/

226 Ramachandra Guha, "A Matter of Personality: Nehru Remembered, and Recovered, by a Not-Wholly-Biased Historian," *The Telegraph*, November 12, 2002. https://www.telegraphindia.com/opinion/a-matter-of-personality-nehru-remembered-and-recovered-by-a-not-wholly-biased-historian/cid/1015672

227 Sita Ram Goel, *Genesis and Growth of Nehruism*, p. 30

228 Harsh Madhusudan and Rajeev Mantri, "Excerpt: A New Idea of India by Harsh Madhusudan and Rajeev Mantri," *Hindustan Times*, 20 September, 2020

229 Ahoka Mody, *India Is Broken*, p. 105

230 Ibid.

231 Jawaharlal Nehru, *Glimpses of World History*, p. 853

232 "The Modern Review Special: Rashtrapati," Indian History Collective. https://indianhistorycollective.com/the-modern-review-special-rashtrapati/

233 Bill of Rights Institute, Federalist Papers No. 10 (1787), available at https://billofrightsinstitute.org/primary-sources/federalist-no-10

234 Ahoka Mody, *India Is Broken*, p. 18

235 Ibid.

236 Katherine Frank, *Indira, The Life of Indira Nehru Gandhi*, p. 302

237 Ashoka Mody, *India Is Broken*, p. 203

238 William Borders, "Mrs Gandhi Calls India Democratic Even Under Curbs," *New York Times*, July 3, 1975

239 Ashoka Mody, *India Is Broken*, pp. 174–75

240 American Economic Journal, https://www.aeaweb.org/articles?id=10.1257/jep.5.1.97

241 Douglass C. North, "Institutions," *Journal of Economic Perspectives*, Vol. 5, no. 1, (Winter 1991), pp. 97–112

URBAN NAXALS: The Making of Buddha In A Traffic Jam

Vivek Agnihotri

978-1942426059 I ₹ 499 I PB

Urban Naxals reveals Vivek Agnihotri's journey to expose the urban network behind India's Maoist insurgency—leftist academia, media, NGOs—through his film's struggle, screenings, and the ideological war that followed.

LOVE JIHAD OR PREDATORY DAWAH?

Monika Arora, Sonali Chitalkar, Shruti Mishra, Monicca Agarwaal

978-1942426639 I ₹ 299 I PB

This book explores interfaith relationships involving Muslims and non-Muslims, revealing real-life stories, legal issues, Sharia conflicts, and ideological motives—questioning whether such alliances are rooted in love, dominance, or religious conversion.

HACK THE BOREDOM CODE

Neera Maini Srivastav

979-8885750677 I ₹ 299 I PB

Hack the Boredom Code is your go-to guide to beat monotony. With humor, insight, and practical ideas, it helps you turn dull moments into joyful discoveries and find meaning in everyday life.

DELHI RIOTS 2020:
The Untold Story

Monika Arora, Sonali Chitalkar, Prerna Malhotra

978-1942426295 I ₹ 299 I PB

Delhi Riots 2020 were a pre-planned, ideologically driven eruption of violence in North East Delhi, orchestrated under the guise of anti-CAA protests, devastating inter-community harmony through targeted attacks, arson, and brutal killings.

About the Author

An alumnus of Columbia Business School, Aarnab Mitra did his schooling and college at St Xavier's, Kolkata. He is a senior journalist and has been the National Editor and National Business Editor of *Hindustan Times*, Deputy Editor of *Business Today*, and Joint News Editor of *The Economic Times*. He has also worked for *The Telegraph* and *The Asian Age* in Kolkata.

In addition to this, Mitra has worked in the corporate sector in Norwegian multinational Statkraft's India country office in a senior role.

Mitra lives in Gurgaon (Haryana) with his wife, daughter, mother and two dogs. He has self-published a novel, *The Dwarf's Moon*, and has written/ghost written the autobiographies of well-known corporate personalities such as Dr U.S. Awasthi of IFFCO, among several others. He has also ghostwritten a book on wealth management by a well-known wealth manager and authored a coffee table book on behalf of the GMR Group on its new Goa airport at Mopa.